Working Class Kinship

Working Class Kinship

George S. Rosenberg
Case Western Reserve University

Donald F. Anspach
University of Maine at Portland-
Gorham

Lexington Books
D.C. Heath and Company
Lexington, Massachusetts
Toronto   London

Library of Congress Cataloging in Publication Data

Rosenberg, George S.   1930-
    Working class kinship.

    Bibliography: p.
    1. Kinship—United States—Case studies.
I. Anspach, Donald F., joint author. II. Title.
HQ535.R65   301.42'1   73-940
ISBN 0-669-86751-9

Published simultaneously in Canada.

Printed in the United States of America.

International Standard Book Number: 0-669-86751-9

Library of Congress Catalog Card Number: 73-940

229524

To Ruth and Allison

Contents

List of Tables

Preface

This book grows out of an interest in patterns of social isolation and social integration in the working class. A previous work (Rosenberg, 1970) concentrated on aspects of the social isolation of urban working class people. This study deals with the same population, but is focused on their integration into systems of kinship relations.

Received wisdom in social stratification pictures working class people as highly familistic, perhaps more so than middle class people. However, the way in which this conclusion has been reached deserves critical attention. Studies purporting to make interclass comparisons as well as those based solely on data about the working class do not have common measures of familism or kinship relations, nor common definitions of who is to be included within the universe of kin of working class people, nor common definitions of what constitutes membership in the working class itself. As a result, a clear picture cannot be formed of the nature of kinship within the working class; and interclass comparisons of family and kinship relations rest on an insecure base.

Thus it happens that controversies rage about matters as diverse as matriarchy and matricentricity in the working class; kinship relations as supportive of, or compensatory for, the working class person who has been unsuccessful in the economy; the composition of families in poverty and recipients of public assistance; the persistence of extra-domiciliary forms of kinship relations in the face of the pressures of modern industrial economies; and so forth. It is probably fair to say, then, that one source of difficulty in arriving at a clear description of the nature of working class kinship, and indeed kinship in general in a contemporary, urban, industrial setting, is a lack of agreement about certain fundamentally definitional matters—a dissensus which has led to competing notions on a wide range of issues.

However, another source of difficulty may be more important in obscuring our view of the nature of kinship relations in the working class, and at other socioeconomic levels as well. Simply put, much of the dissensus which plagues kinship studies stems from inadequate theory of kinship. The domestic unit has been mistaken for the only unit of American kinship. Theorists have not systematically addressed the question of whether American society today possesses a single-core kinship system, perhaps with minor variations, or plural kinship systems, coexisting within a single national state. Too much of the theory of kinship which does exist is the end product of tenuous inference from cultural data such as kinship terminology, to structural features such as patterns of social interaction. All too infrequently do researchers realize that the relationship of cultural to interaction features of kinship is in fact an independent question to be answered by empirical inquiry. And where theory has been informed by empirical research it has been poorly served.

For example, countless studies describe the kind of aid and assistance exchanged by kin, but few systematically explore the degree of kinship relation of those who assist each other. But most important, and underlying all of these theoretical problems with which students of the family and kinship must deal, is the fundamental neglect of the fact that ours is a system of bilateral kinship arrangements. No investigation can afford to ignore the respects in which the structure of the bilateral kinship system influences the recruitment of relatives for social interaction—or, for that matter, any aspect of kinship structure or function. Thus it is that this study examines working class kinship interaction from the point of view of the larger structure of kinship in which it is embedded.

This approach places many traditional problems in a new light, reveals others as false problems, and raises several new questions. Some of these will be discussed at greater length in pages to follow; but perhaps these brief remarks give something of a prefatory indication of the reasons why this work was undertaken. They boil down to the conviction that some of our most cherished notions about the relation between stratification and kinship may be inadequate. Not because of inaccuracy of measurement, failure to study representative samples, or the like, but because our basic terms of discourse and the concepts and theories about the social entities we are dealing with when we talk about kinship are not very illuminating. They do not fit the data we have about kinship very well; they do not allow us to make analytic distinctions among units or sections of kin in ways that resolve important controversies about kinship; and they do not permit us to push very far ahead in answering some central questions about the relationship between kinship and other social institutions, especially the economy.

When the data on which this book is based were gathered it was decided that the proper procedure, in view of these difficulties, was to concentrate first on patterns of interaction. Once these were better known, the next step could be taken—an assessment of the content of interaction and of attendant beliefs and attitudes. Accordingly, the issues of kinship and class we have touched upon here are approached through an analysis of patterns of interaction of working class people and their kin. While we realize the limitations of this focus on interaction, it nevertheless remains one of the best ways available to obtain a perspective on the structure of kinship.

In this study the population from which information on kinship was gathered ranges from middle to old age. A mature population was sampled because of the need to investigate working class people who had already reached their ultimate destination in the economy. Also, it was felt necessary to obtain a better picture of the impact of age and retirement on the various facets of social integration and social isolation with which this study was concerned. The practical consequence of the sampling restriction on age for the present work is a lack of living ascendant kin reported by our respondents. However, since our basic datum is interaction frequency or rate, intergenerational relations among kin are examined through respondents and their contact with descendant kin. If the recruitment of kin for social interaction is anything more than a random social process, its various characteristics and aspects will be visible in analysis, whether we start our investigation from the point of view of the parental or the filial generation.

Many people and institutions have assisted us. Thanks are due to the Social Security Administration (grants 193(1)-5-127 and 193(2)-6-187) for support which enabled George Rosenberg to gather the data on which this study is based. Donald Anspach was assisted in this research by Grant 1-F1-MH-45, 867-01, National Institute of Mental Health, United States Department of Health, Education, and Welfare. Thanks are also due to the editors of *The Journal of Marriage and the Family* for permission to use some material from our article, "Working Class Matricentricity," which appeared in the August 1972 issue. The stimulation we have derived from the comments of numerous colleagues is gratefully acknowledged. Raymond Firth, Leo Despres, and Charles Callender in particular have been helpful from the anthropological point of view. Special thanks are due to Victor Thiessen for writing programs used to analyze kinship data. And for typing the manuscript we are grateful to Letitia Cramer and Linda McKenzie.

Working Class Kinship

1 The Problematics of Kinship

The aim of this book is to provide an alternative to the current, conflicting conceptions of American kinship. The major opposing positions in the debate are exemplified on the one hand by Talcott Parsons and his colleagues, who propound a version of the isolated nuclear family thesis, and on the other hand by Marvin Sussman and Eugene Litwak, who argue for the existence of considerable extra-familial integration of concrete kinship units in contemporary American society. We believe that both these positions are erroneous. Neither of them is successful in explaining the known variability in extra-familial kinship interaction. Neither of them has correctly identified the unit of American kinship, nor described its characteristics. Neither of these chief schools of thought is couched in a clear and unambiguous language of concepts and definitions. Neither have provided a satisfactory base of empirical evidence to support their general statements about American kinship. And neither Parsons nor Sussman and Litwak have succeeded in fitting concept and theory to what we know of the substance of American kinship and family relations.

In the pages that follow, we shall attempt to provide a theoretical framework that we believe offers a viable alternative to those now before us. And we shall support our position with data on kinship interaction in the contemporary, urban working class.

Since this book is essentially an attempt to alter the terms of discourse involved in the controversy over kinship, and since it offers a new and considerably different perspective on these questions, it is necessary at the outset to state our view of the progress of ongoing debate, the facets of controversy which appear to be central, and the respects in which the protagonists seem to have gone awry.

While we offer a new way to conceptualize the problem of kinship in industrial societies, we will not attempt to resolve all the problems which are the subject of controversy—at least, not in the terms in which they are usually cast. For some of them are simply not resolvable; others are false problems, having arisen because parties to debate talked past each other; and still others seem to be fruitless and hence are probably best avoided altogether. Instead, by addressing the issue of recruitment of kin for interaction, we hope to emerge with a new agenda of priorities for the study of the relational system of kinship and reformulate the problem of how extra-familial kin ties should be viewed. But first, a look at the controversy which has shaped so much of the thinking about kinship in our society.

1

The Question of Isolation

It is only within the past two decades that kinship has received systematic attention by American sociologists. Previous studies have stressed the importance of the nuclear family to the comparative neglect of its surrounding social network of friends, neighbors, and in particular, relatives. This view was typified by Margaret Mead (1948) when she spoke of the tiny biological family of the modern American three-room-apartment dwellers who have no kin within a thousand miles.

This past lack of attention paid to the study of extra-familial kin ties, exemplified in Mead's opinion about the family, has several sources, not the least of which is the fact that in terms of social perception the household juts out in prominence whereas other kin units do not. The household as a family domicile is the only major, concrete kin group in our society. It is a highly discrete unit in residence, in property holdings, income control, and in social affairs (Firth, 1956:13).[a]

The initial controversy over kinship concerns characteristics of kinship systems in modern, urban-industrial societies. A major aspect of this debate centers on the claim that the nuclear family has become isolated from a wide range of kin as a function of its changing economic position, which stems from the industrial revolution and the change in family composition to the conjugal form of husband, wife, and children.

This debate has its origins in the work of Talcott Parsons. Parsons was not the first to recognize differences among kinship systems in industrialized and nonindustrialized societies. He was not the first to proclaim that the conjugal family was more isolated from other units of kinship in the urban milieux. Nor indeed was he the first to see the implications of the differentiation of kinship from economic organization. Such insights were ones which Parsons was able to adopt from a wide variety of sources. However, what is distinctive—and of major importance in Parsons—is the part that is given to a theory of kinship within his total theoretical system. Parsons' perspective on kinship, which is elaborated in some detail, is closely interrelated with a number of other analyses so that it becomes a crucial element in his entire construction.

For example, in Parsons the differentiation of the economy from kinship and the organization of the former along rational, universalistic principles is a major process involved in enhancing a society's adaptive capacity. It is in this sense that the structural isolation of kinship from the economy is an essential ingredient in his evolutionary schema. Again, kinship is of central significance in Parsons' approach to stratification. Indeed, at one point he formulates the idea of stratification as the dimension of society which results from the organization of the economy and the family. In this context the determination of occupational status by family connections would threaten the universalistic criteria which are

---

[a]For this and all other author references, see the Bibliography.

critical for the system as a whole. The isolation of the nuclear family is then the mechanism that frees the occupational member of the family from ties that would interfere with the operation of the stratification system. Moreover, it may be noted that Parsons' analysis of achievement and consequent social mobility is predicated on the notion that the isolation of the conjugal family has significantly reduced the ascription of status by family origin. The occupational system and its structural correlates place severe limitations on the kinds of kinship organizations which are compatible with it, according to Parsons.

Additional support for the thesis of the isolation of the nuclear family is provided by the way our kinship system articulates with the systems of mate choice and marriage. Since our kinship system fails to provide anyone with a stable position in any kin group other than the nuclear family, Parsons (1943:30) argues that the marriage bond becomes the most important kinship loyalty and that the marriage relationship assumes the greatest structural significance. The importance placed on the marriage relation in turn makes our system of mate selection an open one in which mate choice is ideally based on mutual attraction. The kinship system's articulation with the systems of mate choice and marriage in turn reinforces the conjugal pair's independence from kin because it lessens the obligations that could develop with other relatives.

Thus the thesis of the structural isolation of the nuclear family has led to the description of our kinship system by Parsons, Goode, and others as a conjugal family system. The most important features of the conjugal family construct are the emphasis on the solidarity of the marriage bond and the relative exclusion of a wide range of kin from the conjugal family's everyday affairs (Goode, 1963:9). Since there is no great extension of the kin network, the couple cannot rely upon a large number of relatives for help, just as these relatives cannot call upon the couple for help. Since kin ties are weak, the residential location of the couple is not greatly determined by kin.

Thus it is not difficult to appreciate why kinship in industrial societies has almost invariably been an important question, and why successive examinations of the place of the family and kinship in industrial society have regularly taken Parsons as an important point of reference. Some of the basic questions which have been examined are: To what extent are individuals geographically and socially isolated from a wide range of kin? Does occupational advancement or decline isolate individuals from their relatives? To what extent is occupational status determined by family connection? Such issues have in fact been under continuous and usually intense discussion virtually from 1943, the time when Parsons' seminal paper, "The Kinship System of the Contemporary United States," first appeared. To illustrate with an issue of particular interest here, the question of the significance of kin ties outside the household was initially examined in the 1950s through the empirical studies of Axelrod and Sharp (1956) and of Sussman (1959). In looking at leisure activities of working class people, Axelrod and Sharp (1956) and Dotson (1951) found that visiting among relatives was an important social activity and in some cases the only leisure activity in which these people engaged. Sussman has found that the household group is not isolated from kin but functions within a kin network of component kin-related households. The relationships between adult children and their parents is especially strong, as evidenced by the amount of help and aid flowing between them.

These findings, it may be observed, are subsequently incorporated by Parsons into his total system schema. Characteristically, Parsons (1968:38) states:

To my mind the two views are not contradictory but complementary. The concept isolation applies in the first instance to kinship structure seen in the perspective of anthropological studies in that field. In this context, our system represents an extreme type which is well described by that term. It does not, however, follow that all relations to kin outside the nuclear family are broken. Indeed the very psychological importance for the individual of the nuclear family in which he was born and brought up would make any such conception impossible.

Thus Parsons does not use isolation to mean absence of contact among kin, but rather to mean that the most stringent obligations to kin occur within the household and that contacts with kin outside this unit are subordinated to its needs (Parsons, 1951:186; Pitts, 1964:89). And, there is some question whether findings such as Sussman's, of contact among kin, necessarily point to any inadequacy in the Parsonian system. Parsons' thesis of isolation must be understood not only within the context of his analysis of the interrelations between the family and the economy, but also within the context of his analysis of the American kinship system as well.

The weight of much of Parsons' argument is based on the analysis of the American kinship system. Taking the cultural-terminological system as the point of departure, Parsons stated that our kinship system operates in terms of principles of bilateral descent in the first ascending and descending generations, and as multilineal in succeeding generations—meaning that descent (and hence kinship relation) is reckoned on both sides of ego's nuclear family and that any number of lines of descent may be treated as significant. Second, Parsons sees this system of descent as symmetrical, meaning that there is no terminological or structural bias favoring solidarity with ascendants or descendants in any one line of descent, thus making an "onion structure" the most distinctive feature of the kinship system. Third, on the basis that there are no recognized kinship units (or groups of relatives) cutting across the nuclear family or involving its members, Parsons concluded that the American kinship system is made up exclusively of interlocking nuclear families, and that the isolated nuclear family is the major structural unit of American kinship.

Parsons' use of terminological analysis is one way of studying kinship. However, the approach limits his statements to those that can be made about kinship as a cultural system. He sees kinship from the point of view of the cultural system and thus is not directly concerned with behavior and interaction among kin. Moreover, as Adams (1968:177) has correctly stated, Parsons is interested in the comparative and historical problem of the place of the American kinship system in society and its relationship with other societal systems. And, as Mirande (1968:153) notes, Parsons' hypothesis of the isolated family proposes that the family in American society is relatively isolated (relative, that is, to families in less urbanized and industrialized societies).

Despite the differences in both approach and perspective among the opponents in this debate, the continuing lack of validation for Parsons' theory of isolation from kin encouraged more critical appraisals. These criticisms were attempts to identify particular deficiencies in his analysis, and may be summarized as three separate but related arguments:

1. The isolated family hypothesis is elaborated in a framework that utilizes the vitality of the extended family found in some primitive societies as a pseudo-comparison group. But, students of predominately agricultural societies have not found that these people's ties with kin are markedly strong, as was previously thought (Petersen, 1969:271).

2. Industrialization is not a cause of the dissolution of extended families and the consequent isolation from kin. Greenfield (1961:316) has found that small nuclear families can exist without industrialization and urbanization, and the latter can exist without small domestic groups. He states that there is no necessary and sufficient relation between the two. And, Petersen (1969:271) claims that we still do not know whether kin networks in preindustrial and developing societies do or do not tend to be larger, more extended, and more active than kin networks in urban, highly industrialized societies.

3. Finally, there are those who argue that Parsons' position is tenable only if one accepts as given the thesis that urbanization and industrialization are accompanied by social and moral upheaval. As evidence accumulates, there is reason to suggest that this thesis is more a matter of assumption than of fact. In the first place, the disruption of extra-familial kin ties may be a temporary process which occurs only during periods of emerging industrialization. Thus Parsons' claim would hold true only during the short period of time when migrations relocate large numbers of people in a society. In this vein, Key (1961:56) suggests that once the immigrants to the cities have the opportunity to establish families, extra-familial kin ties are revitalized and adapted to the urban milieux. In fact he suggests that the impersonality of the city probably increases effective ties with kin. Firth (1964:83) also argues that personal kin ties not only are retained but may be strengthened by industrial, urban conditions.

Lacking cross-cultural or historical proof supporting or refuting Parsons' claim, students of the family turned to the relationship between social mobility and extended family cohesion as an indirect test of his thesis. While the underlying logic of this approach is sound, suggesting that Parsons' thesis indicates that mobile families would have fewer relationships with kin than nonmobile families, the findings are still inconclusive. Although Litwak (1960) has shown that extra-familial kin support mobility through various forms of aid and help, evidence exists demonstrating that mobility has an attenuating effect on kin ties, through the geographical disperson of kin (Adams, 1968) and reduction in contact (Mirande, 1968) as well.

Critique of Concepts and Units of Analysis

This then was the stage which the debate over the isolated nuclear family had reached by the 1960s. Following one or more of these lines of attack, an alternative to Parsons' model was made possible. Research during this period primarily focused on various contributions that relatives provided each other in the form of aid and help on occasions of crisis and rites of passage. According to Adams (1968:51) no other single aspect of urban kinship has received more attention than the mutual aid that flows between relatives.

It is important to recognize that the controversy over isolation that we have been discussing involves, among other things, confusion about two related but analytically distinct aspects of kinship: normative and relational. As noted above, Parsons is primarily concerned with the normative dimension of kinship and has approached the problem from a terminological point of view, while Sussman and others are concerned with kinship relations and have approached the problem from a structural point of view in identifying regularities in patterns of behavior. Our stance toward Parsons' approach, as well as toward that of his opponents, is neither assent nor dissent. We take the position that the relationship of cultural to structural units is an empirical question—that Parsons's approach and that of his opponents are both valid ways to study kinship, and yet they do not result in isomorphic pictures of kinship systems because they focus on different dimensions of a complex entity.

However, we do maintain that while both have a tenuous hold on different but related aspects of the problem, the still unconsolidated and somewhat irreconcilable collection of partial explanations does indicate a major gap in kinship theory. Current conceptualization is simply inadequate.

This may be demonstrated in a number of ways. For example, consider the terms employed to designate units of kinship. There is confusion over three separate analytic meanings of the term nuclear family: as a concrete residence unit; as a particular structural type; and as an invariant set of functions. Noting these problems, Levy and Fallers (1959) and Lancaster (1961) suggest the use of the concept "kin-structured domestic unit" as an alternative to the nuclear family. To take another example, the term "kin network" is vague and imprecise, as it points to the existence of social relations with kin in an amorphous way by failing to delineate which relatives are involved or how such relationships vary in different contexts.

Perhaps the most serious conceptual problem is Litwak's use of the "modified extended family." In order to demonstrate that kin relations exist outside the domestic unit and at the same time attempting to delineate a theoretical model that fits the industrial and urban nature of our society, Litwak proposes that a modified form of the classic extended family is more valid than Parsons' isolated nuclear family construct. According to Litwak (1965:291), the modified extended family neither requires people to establish proximate residence on the basis of kinship nor does it require the introduction of nepotistic norms within bureaucracy. However, it does permit the nuclear family household to remain active with other kin in situations where extended family aid can be given.

Litwak has used the concept of the modified extended family where it has questionable applicability. There is no evidence that the classic extended family existed in our recent or distant past. Goode (1963:6-7) argues that extended families were not common and adds that while most houses were small they were also poorly constructed; thus, the exceptionally well built (though untypical) larger ones remained, resulting in a historical distortion of our perception of the family's size and composition. Parsons also agrees that extended families were not a part of our heritage. According to him (1943:38), it is safe to assume that conjugal families and the corresponding absence of groupings of kin cutting across them have existed in western society since the period in which the kinship terminology of the European languages took shape!

Moreover, the concept of the extended family, rigorously construed, is a structural one used to study kin groupings where residence rules favor a composite form of the family (Murdock, 1949:Chapter 1). As defined by Lancaster (1961:328), employing a standard definition from *Notes and Queries on Anthropology*, the extended family refers to a kin unit, not necessarily living in the same household, in which two or more lineally related kin of the same sex, with their spouses and offspring, are subject to a single head with jural authority.

Now as a tool for studying American kinship structure, Litwak (1959-1960:177-178) defines the modified extended family structure as a series of nuclear families (i.e., units of residence) joined together on an equalitarian basis for mutual aid. The concept as construed by Litwak is an attempt to indicate that there is regularity in kin relations outside the domestic unit. It does not specify which relatives are involved and is thus in no way analogous to the rigorous anthropological meaning of the concept. One must then question the use of Litwak's concept for the study of kinship. It probably should be dropped from the analysis of American kinship structure because for this purpose it is meaningless as Litwak defines it.

Furthermore, any analytic apparatus used to study kinship relations in our society must not only account in some way for the requisites of urbanization and industrialization, but must also be congruent with the structure of our kinship system. A major characteristic of bilateral kinship systems, considered cross-culturally, is the absence of residence rules that favor this composite form of the family. In his cross-cultural study, Murdock (1968:255) did not find extended families in societies with bilateral kinship systems. Mogey (1964:506) notes that it is erroneous to attempt to derive the modern family from the extended family because it has (as noted) a dubious historical existence in western societies.

Thus it is clear that much of the contemporary study of the relational aspect of kinship lacks analytically precise concepts. It is also clear that the decade of research characterized by the dispute with Parsons' thesis of isolation was guided by these concepts rather than directed at questioning them. Partially because of this confusion in conceptualization, Gibson (1972:13) suggests that the case for the vitality and functionality of the kin network has yet to be proved. This may or may not be true. At the least, he has demonstrated that Sussman's evidential base fails to support the claimed conception of extra-familial kin structure. But as we shall show later in this chapter and throughout this book, it is a fruitless issue in the terms in which Gibson and others have couched it.

Now we must raise another question: Have we been studying kinship at all, or have we been studying family forms and relations between domestic groups? The question arises because of the prevailing tendency to look at kinship relations by examining how families interact and associate with one another. What, then, is the system of reference when the domestic group is used as the unit of analysis? At the heart of the matter is the distinction between approaches to domestic groupings where the nuclear family is used as the basis upon which more complex forms are compounded, and approaches that use nuclear family roles as a point of departure for the analysis of kinship. In the latter, a clear distinction is made between the domestic group and an individual's nuclear family roles. An individual's—ego's—relationship to nuclear kin is examined, followed by an examination of his relationships with more distant, nonnuclear kin (Murdock, 1949:91-122; 204).

The first approach examines relationships between groups; the second examines an individual's relationships with kin. The unit of analysis in the former is the household, while that of the latter is the individual. Both are valid ways of examining kinship structure and must be seen as complementary. The choice of approach clearly depends on the problem under investigation. The household approach directs attention to patterns of visiting and types of aid and support given and received among kin-related domestic units. However, it is limited because it does not permit consideration of possible differences among individuals who comprise the household in their relationships with kin. The ego-centered approach is limited with respect to examining the total pattern of visiting and help given and received by a household, but has the advantage of examining possible differences among individuals in their relationships with kin. This approach directs attention to the question of variability in relationships with kin and the choices an individual makes among kin in deciding with whom to establish or maintain social relationships.

By using the household or domestic group as the unit of analysis, Litwak, Sussman, and others have placed the focus of attention on relationships between groups. Although this is a valid approach to the study of groupings of relatives formed on a kinship basis, it can be misleading in the study of kinship in our society. Many different groupings of people can be recruited on the basis of kinship, such as lineages, clans, and extended families. In our society the only major kin grouping is the domestic unit, ideally composed of nuclear family roles (Cumming and Schneider, 1961:499).

In view of problems such as these, Loudon (1961:335) suggests the use of the ego-centered approach, focusing on the individual and his relationships with kin, as an alternative to the household approach, which focuses on composite family forms. Research using the ego-centered approach points to differences between men and women, between spouses, and between parents and children in the degree of recognition and extent of contact with kin not living in the household.

A reorientation to the study of kinship is implicit in much of what we have been discussing. It is no longer a question of whether Parsons' or some other model currently available is correct, but rather a question of posing the problem anew. This ultimately involves specification of the type of kinship structure—rather than family structure—which is compatible with characteristics of urban industrial societies and which comports with characteristics of bilateral kinship systems as well. One must question the utility of such notions as isolated family, kin network, and extended family for future studies of kinship. While the research that flowed from their use served the heuristic purpose of focusing attention on the ubiquitous small domestic unit and its relation to a wider network of kin, these notions are no longer adequate for the range of facts to which they should be expected to apply.

It may be observed that inadequate and misleading theory and concepts— theory and concepts that fail to account for the complexity of normative and relational dimensions of kinship systems in urban and industrial settings—is a state of affairs that has arisen from a curious paradox. While descriptive studies show that Americans are neither isolated from relatives interactionally, geo- graphically, attitudinally, nor in terms of kinship knowledge, nevertheless, proponents of the isolation-of-the-family thesis are led to underscore the absence of any group of relatives with jural status other than the household. They point out that many traditional functions of kinship are absent, as well as noting that the composition of households are ideally and modally comprised of nuclear family roles; hence they reject the modified extended family construct. How- ever, as previously noted, this paradox is more apparent than real since the statements apply to different aspects of a complex entity. Although no concrete formal grouping of relatives exists outside the household, relations with extra-familial kin do remain on a selective basis and play an important role in expressive spheres of activity.

Thus, while extra-familial kinship is a major structural feature of urban, industrial society, the systematic study of the structure and function of kinship—as distinct from the family—has received little attention. We have more knowledge of patterns of aid and support given and received among kin than we have of which kin are involved or how these relationships vary in different contexts. According to Robins and Tomanec (1962:340), few studies (1) have presented evidence concerning the conditions under which bonds with kin not living within the household are maintained; (2) have attempted to test the extent to which Parsons' ideally symmetrical pattern with respect to line of descent is followed in actual practice; or (3) have sought to determine the norms governing the selection among available kin of those with whom to maintain reciprocal performances of services or demonstrations of concern and affection.

The Relational System of Extra-Familial Kin Ties

Thus at the end of a decade of research on American kinship we were in a position to reject the thesis that few if any social relations with kin occurred, as well as its corollary that those which did occur lacked any importance at all. Beyond this, however, little else was known.

We were not in a position to assess the importance of kin ties. The question of the minimal level of activity needed among kin to provide an adequate basis for a social relationship could not be, and was not, raised until 1965, when Rosow stated the issue fairly clearly. According to him (1965:375), ritual visitations, ceremonial observances, and assistance are not at all synonymous with continual contact among kin; and it was precisely on this basis that attempts were made to refute the isolation thesis.

But the perplexing problem remained of determining whether any structure of extra-familial kin ties could be identified at all. We knew that personal kin ties outside the familial-domiciliary unit did not constitute a concrete, formal group of relatives with binding obligations upon one another, nor was it a constituent unit of social structure. While social relations occurred among kin, these ties seemed so loose as to lack any identity at all. In recognizing this issue, Firth (1956:12) suggested that it was not the supposed low level of activity occurring among extra-familial kin but the variability in behavior among kin that accounted for our failure to come to grips with this issue.

Research conducted in the sixties clearly demonstrates that variability in behavior among kin is the problem which must be accounted for before any model of kinship can be fully developed. Cumming and Schneider, for example, found this issue to be central in kinship reckoning. According to them (1961:499) the number of kin their informants recognized ranged from 34 to 280, with a median of 152. The number of people these informants knew who occupied the kinship roles they identified varied as well. And the number of relatives whose first names respondents could give was about half the number they recognized.

This pattern of variability is not limited to reckoning of kin. Cumming and Schneider (1961:501) did not find that informant's feelings of intimacy were connected to genealogical distance. For example, parents were excluded from what some informants considered intimate kin; others gave the same status to a sibling's child as to his own child. No category of kin was specifically favored for interaction. In cases of geographical propinquity, selectivity was based on compatibility. Geographically distant kin were seen as a reserve available for selection when the opportunity arose. Findings of variability along these lines also have been reported by Adams (1968), Schneider (1968), Gibson (1972), and others.

Variability in the extent to which individuals recognize people as kin, contact their kin, and variability in which relatives are seen remain central issues in the study of contemporary kinship. While research has consistently shown that social relations occur among extra-familial kin, the problem has become one of identifying factors that explain variability in kinship relations. Variations in the level of activity occurring among kin have not been tied to explanatory variables, and as a consequence, conceptual models have not been developed.

Any conceptual framework that reformulates the problem of kinship in urban-industrial society must take the variability found in kinship behavior as in itself problematic. But by and large this has not been done. The issue of variability has been construed as a given by some—variability has been thought of as a property inherent in the kinship system itself. This is particularly evident in the more recent work of Parsons, and Cumming and Schneider, receiving final elaboration in Schneider's (1968) *American Kinship: A Cultural Account.*

For example, in accounting for social relationships among kin, Parsons claimed that there is an optional-permissive quality of the expectation system. According to him (1968:39):

There certainly are some structured preferences on kinship bases, and others on those of geographical propinquity, but still there is a strong tendency for kinship to shade into friendship in the sense of absence from the latter of ascriptive components of membership. Hence, the amount of visiting, of common activity, of telephone and written communication, etc., is highly variable within formal categories of (kin) relationship.

Thus Parsons suggests that the variability in kinship behavior is accounted for by the kinship system itself, which makes relationships with kin permissive by virtue of the fact that they lack ascriptive qualities.

Or as Schneider has it, the variability in recognition of kin, and in the nature of relationships established with kin, is to be interpreted as characteristic of a kinship system whose rules provide for latitude of choice. According to Schneider (1968:114), the variability in the range of recognized kin in the United States is not due to the presence of different kinship systems, but to a single-core kinship system, which itself permits an individual latitude in whether to recognize some people as kin and gives people a further choice in whether to establish social relationships with kin on the basis of known kinship links.

The variability and latitude permitted in selecting kin for interaction in turn has been seen as reflecting a certain looseness in the kinship system that fits equalitarian values of the society while at the same time permitting social relationships among kin to be used for a variety of purposes and accommodate occasional as well as sustained levels of interaction. Relationships occurring among kin in our society are characterized by Parsons (1965), Cumming and Schneider (1961), and Schneider (1968) as involving the expression of diffuse solidarity in a variety of ways. According to Farber (1964:196), kin interaction includes participation in rituals and ceremonies, promoting the welfare of family members, and the open communication between and concerning relatives which is necessary for intimacy, trust, and other characteristics of primariness.

The open-choice perspective on kinship presented by these authors suggests that the relational system is important to individuals and in this way significant, but lacks an identifiable structure of interrelated statuses and roles. They suggest that since kinship roles outside the household are not treated differentially for purposes of interaction, permissiveness in establishing and maintaining social relations with kin is inherent in the system itself. Moreover, this view suggests that if kinship norms are operative, they are not distinct but merge imperceptibly with those of friendship.

Schneider elaborated this perspective by suggesting that sentiments of kinship are not in themselves a sufficient basis for establishing or continuing social relationships with kin. According to him (1968:75-76), a most important fact in our society is that a relative is first of all a person. His standing as a relative is only one component of his status set. If he is considered to be socially significant, it is probably because of attributes of the person other than those connected with kinship. From Schneider's perspective, the selection of kin with whom to interact has little to do with genealogical considerations of kinship, but instead is related to a multiplicity of factors that include geographical dispersion and propinquity among kin, and socioemotional factors as well. How factors such as these influence the selection of kin is in turn related to class, age, and sex-related variables.

As viewed by these authors, then, choice is built into the relational system of kinship in American society. In fact it appears to be its defining characteristic. Since a high degree of variability and selectivity are characteristic of the system portrayed by them, social relationships that do occur depend on nonkinship characteristics of both the individual and his relatives.

The approach developed by these authors does not comport with Sussman and Litwak's conceptualization of extra-familial kin ties. The kin network and modified extended family concepts of Sussman and Litwak suggest that a system of interrelated statuses and roles exist which are differentiated by considerations of genealogical distance and which are governed to a considerable extent by distinct kinship norms. Parsons, Cumming, and Schneider play these factors down in their portrayal of a system whose norms are so permissive that they provide almost complete latitude in the choice of which relatives are contacted by an individual.

We disagree with the points of view presented in both these schools of thought. Rather, we submit that both sets of authors have failed to successfully address the basic issue of accounting for variability in kinship behavior. While the kin network and modified extended family concepts do not fit the variability found in kin interaction, the alternative of making variability all but random and inherent in the system begs the question. Moreover, we have argued that any model of kinship must fit with the characteristics of our particular type of kinship system as well. The perspectives on relational aspects of kinship developed by Sussman and Litwak on the one hand, and Cumming, Parsons, and Schneider on the other, simply do not mesh well with the bilateral character of our kinship system as it exists in contemporary, urban, industrial societies.

If we accept the question of variability in kinship interaction as an important issue, then the basis on which an individual chooses which relatives to see becomes of primary theoretical interest. By posing the question in this way, we can examine the extent to which nonkinship criteria are important in recruitment, and determine whether kinship norms are in operation as well.

In order to reformulate the problematics of kinship along these lines, additional information is needed on the nature of bilateral kinship systems, of which ours is an example. That is, it is necessary to spell out some of the characteristics common to our system and to other bilateral kinship systems, and to examine the implications that flow from these similarities. In particular we should be sensitive to the question of the possible range of forms of social organization of kin that could develop outside the household in bilateral kinship systems. In so doing, it will become evident that the role the bilateral character of the kinship system plays in extra-familial kin interaction has not been given sufficient weight.

Bilateral kinship systems are widespread among the societies of the world (Murdock, 1968:236), and are found in societies ranging in technology from simple hunting and gathering, through tilling societies, to European and Asian societies of the highest technological-economic complexity (Zelditch, 1964:490). Regardless of the degree of socioeconomic complexity in such societies, Murdock (1968:253) found several characteristics common to all bilateral systems. These include the presence of small domestic units, neolocal (or ambilocal) residence, and an aggregate of relatives outside this unit referred to as the *kindred*. This extra-familial unit is of particular concern here.

By examining characteristics of the kindred we will be able to view relationships that do occur among relatives in our society, in a perspective consistent with the nature of our kinship system. Furthermore, by making some small modification of the concept of the kindred so that it may better fit with the way kinship appears to be articulated with other subsystems of our society, we will be in a position to bring a new theoretical orientation to bear on the study of kinship interaction and social structure in the contemporary, urban, industrial situation.

According to Murdock (1968:237), in a large number of societies characterized as having bilateral kinship systems, the only grouping of kin other than the dominant domestic unit is the aggregate of relatives to which Rivers (1924:16) gave the name "kindred." The kindred consist of those socially recognized, consanguinal relatives (regardless of sex) with whom an individual has some duties or claims. Murdock (1968:242) believes the kindred to be an occasional kin grouping in almost every society in which they are found. In most societies the *entire* kindred are operative only on occasions of crisis and at rites of passage in the life cycle of the individual to whom they are related. However, social relationships with various representatives of one's kindred do occur on a continual basis.

With these considerations in mind, we can see that the American kinship system may not be related to the wider social structure as a unique function of urbanization and industrialization specifically. Rather, this relation is probably a special case of the general way that bilateral kinship systems articulate with the social structure in any society. The crucial question is whether there is any viable category of kin consonant with adaptability in industrialized, urbanized societies that is, at the same time, consistent with characteristics of bilateral kinship systems. Consideration of recent conceptual refinements of the concept of the kindred, and application of these ideas to our own society, will contribute to the emerging formulation of the nature of such a category of kin; and furthermore, such consideration will permit us to pose the question of variability in social relationships with kin in a more fruitful and productive way.

The Kindred as a Unit of American Kinship

Rivers (1924:16) introduced the concept of kindred into the mainstream of anthropological kinship theory. It is commonly discussed as a structural feature of bilateral kinship systems and has been identified in societies characterized by varying degrees of socioeconomic complexity. The kindred has been used in discussion of American kinship, but the usage has been vague. Kindred has been equated with kin relations, a gathering of relatives, a descent grouping, and kinship ties.

While this muddling limits the possible usefulness of the concept, recent reconsiderations of the concept by Murdock (1968), Lancaster (1959), Freeman (1961), Mitchell (1963), and Fox (1967) are more helpful. They have resurrected the concept and given it relatively precise analytical meaning. On the basis of their refinements we will be able to place the relational system of kinship in an appropriate perspective. (Incidentally, we are aware of anthropological criticism of the use of the concept of kindred as involving substantial ambiguity. However, as we shall show in the following pages, the virtues of the concept and its utility in the analysis of American kinship appear to us to outweigh the objections which have been leveled against it.)

The kindred is defined as a unit of kinship consisting of all an individual's (or ego's) socially significant bilateral kin (Freeman, 1961:198). It consists of persons related to ego other than by marriage. If ego is married, his spouse's kindred are specifically excluded (Freeman, 1961:198), and the spouses of ego's bilateral kin are also excluded. Although the range of effective bilateral kindred who may be recruited for interaction depends in a practical sense on how far an individual traces his kin, the kindred may consist of only a fraction of these relatives (Freeman, 1961:207). The kindred is composed of those bilateral kin who are recognized by ego as having some duties toward and claims on him (Fox, 1967:167). Not all representatives of the kindred may know or be known to each other. Kindred is a category—not a group—defined by the person who is the focal point: kindred come into and out of existence as focal egos are born and die (Fox, 1967:167; Freeman, 1961:207).

There is consensus on the following characteristics of the kindred (Mitchell, 1963:314-350): (1) The kindred is an ego-centered category of relatives; this means that relatives are selected for interaction on the basis of their kinship relation to ego, rather than their and ego's relationship with an ancestor. (2) Every person in a society could have an effective category of kindred; the composition of each category, however, would be specific to the individual. (3) The kindred can only be the same in role composition for siblings—ego's kindred are necessarily different from his mother's or his father's kindred. (4) Kindred endlessly overlap, and for each individual the boundaries are undefined and shifting. (5) The kindred is not a corporate group—though some of the members may form such a group—and it cannot be a constituent unit of social structure with jural status. (6) The kindred is not a group and is never a residential unit. Ethnographic evidence supports the view that it is rare that all members of ego's kindred emerge in group action.

The stage of ego's life cycle can be an important factor in determining which representatives of the kindred are considered to be more important to him. Mitchell (1963:350) suggests that, as a child, the socially effective kindred revolve around the maternal and paternal aggregate of kin; in later life the focus is on his descendants, collaterals, and his collaterals' descendants as the socially significant kin.

The kindred, then, refers to *an individual's socially effective bilateral kin.* The concept provides an appropriate description of the relational system of kinship in societies with bilateral kinship systems. For unlike unilineal kinship systems, the question of choice of kin for interaction in bilateral systems is an important one, as Lancaster (1961:324) has noted. And the concept of the kindred provides a means of resolving the issue of choice without excluding the possibility that the kinship system has a bearing on how these choices are made. According to Freeman (1961:210), some degree of gradation in obligations within the kindred is usual and is related to genealogical distance. However, she adds that kindred relations are not dominated by this notion of gradation. According to her (1961:210), "an even more important feature of the kindred in bilateral societies is that it presents the individual with a wide range of optative relationships—relationships which, in in the absence of any binding descent principle, it is possible for him to accentuate as he pleases or as suits his special interests." Since an individual's socially effective kindred are then situationally selected, Freeman poses the crucial comparative problem (1961:208): What economic and other factors result in variations in the size and composition of kindred from one bilateral society to another?

Whether the relational system of kinship in American society is similar in structural type to identified bilateral kindred in other societies and operates as they do is an empirical rather than a theoretical question. But since the kindred has been found in societies with bilateral kinship systems, it does provide a construct which is appropriate and fitting to the empirical study of variability in kinship behavior. The kindred permits the variability found in social relationships among kin in bilateral kinship systems to be viewed as problematic. For it places theoretical importance on the basis of the selection individuals make in these societies in establishing and maintaining relationships with their relatives. As previously discussed, the modified extended family construct does not have this advantage: it does not fit the characteristics of our kinship system. And, the absence of kinship norms which has been posited by others as inherent in the system begs the question of how kinship enters into these choices. (Whether the kindred model of the relational system of kinship is compatible with characteristics of the urbanized and industrialized nature of our society is a question that will be presently discussed.)

Any model used as an aid in studying the relational system of kinship in our society must take into account the differentiation of the economy from kinship and the regulation along universalistic criteria of activities involved in the economy. At least the kinship structure must be conceived so that it does not in principle hinder the individual's participation in the economic system. The concept "kindred" is compatible with this requirement. That kindred relations are optative to some extent is a fact of fundamental importance in this regard. While moral obligations among kindred arise from the recognition of common descent, few legal obligations exist. Thus, informal relations with kindred may provide potential rewards for the individual around whom such kin are focused, but the kindred do not have jural or corporate status and cannot bring binding legal sanctions to bear on the individual. Since the kindred is not a constituent unit of social structure, it neither precludes ego's nor his kin's participation in other societal subsystems.

The absence of a binding descent principle and the multilineal character of the kinship system means that relations with kin are not culturally determined and thus not obligatory in this sense. This also fits well with the idea of the kindred. As Freeman (1961:210) notes, the cessation of contact with kindred, for whatever reasons, tends to terminate one's relationships and ongoing obligations towards them. This *de facto* rather than *de jure* termination of relations is significant inasmuch as it can free the individual from total domination by the constraints and obligations that could be imposed on a kinship basis. For example, the effect of geographical mobility would be different in societies characterized by kindred rather than descent groups. In the former, geographical mobility could be associated with the attenuation of some kin ties and with the revival of dormant kin ties. However in societies where the kinship system permits descent groups to develop, as Zelditch notes (1964:495), geographical mobility does not necessarily change people's loyalties and contributions to them.

The fact that the kindred is an ego-centered category of kin rather than ancestor-based clearly indicates that the solidarity of extra-familial kin ties may depend on characteristics of the focal individual, or of his relatives, as well as the nature of their kinship relation to each other, rather than on corporate norms of concrete kin groups exclusively. This optative character of the kindred permits the continuation or cessation of social relations with kin to occur on the basis of nonkinship situational criteria while still not ruling out some kinship criteria of social interaction.

Not only does the ego-centeredness of the kindred comport with Firth's view that variability is a major characteristic of the system, it also suggests one of the ways in which this variability can be explained. For a major characteristic of the kindred is that the stage of ego's life cycle is significant in determining which representatives of the kindred are emphasized; and furthermore, it suggests that kin relations change throughout the life cycle. Thus the choice of relatives an individual considers socially significant may be understood in part by knowing where he and his kin are located in the life cycle. Perhaps this explains why Cumming and Schneider (1961:205) found a shift in solidarity over time between individuals and their kin. They report that their older respondents felt closer to their siblings than did younger respondents.

The concept of the kindred seems promising because it not only fits with features of this society, but also is in harmony with much of the description we have of the relational system of kinship as a functioning social subsystem. In this way it is clearly more advantageous than other current models and concepts employed in studying American kinship.

Affines and Kindred

Notwithstanding the fit of the concept of the kindred with contemporary American kinship, it is limited in applicability to relationships with consanguines: inlaws are specifically omitted from this category of relatives. This raises the question of how to incorporate ego's relationships with affines—both his spouse's kindred and their in-marrying affines, and in-marrying affines of his own kindred—into the analysis of kinship from the point of view of the kindred model. The normative emphasis on the solidarity of the conjugal bond suggests that husbands and wives may share a joint kinship universe that would include their respective kindred and the spouses of these relatives. In this sense, affines may provide an important basis of social relations, relations that in some cases may be closer than those between an individual and some members of his own kindred. This requires modification of the traditional view of kindred-based kinship systems.

Existing evidence indicates that kin ties by marriage are also a basis for social relations and that affines are often integrated into the focal individual's network of kin (Komarovsky, 1956; Young and Wilmott, 1957; Rosser and Harris, 1961). However, our understanding of the nature of affinal relationships and how they may resemble or differ from kindred relations has been severely hampered. As Turner (1969:21) points out, this area of kinship has been virtually ignored. Most studies of urban kinship focus on social relationships that occur between the sampled respondents and their own bilateral kin. And most of the studies which have included inlaws within their enumeration of relatives have not treated these kin separately. Affinal relations are a relatively little known area in which more research is required. However, what empirical data and theory do exist may make it possible to suggest an appropriate perspective towards social relationships with affines, and a way of linking the analysis of consanguineous kin and affines in a common approach.

The norms of our society prescribe marriage as a union between individuals rather than a linking of kin groups. While this may be a condition that frees individuals from constraints of kinship, it places a great deal of stress on the conjugal bond. Relative to other kin ties, the marital bond is critical and is thus supported by a cultural emphasis on romantic love. The cultural emphasis on the marriage relation has led Parsons, Goode, and others to describe our kinship system as a series of interlocking nuclear families. The ideal norms of our society are such that the husband and wife share their relatives and act together in kin affairs. For example, as Komarovsky argues (1962:244-245), married people are expected to treat their own and their spouses' kindred equally for interaction. It is in this ideal-cultural sense that Parsons claims that the nuclear family is a unit within the kinship system.

However, there may be variation in the extent to which this prescript is generally realized within a society, or variation in level within the kinship system at which the ideal is approximated. One kindred may be emphasized for interaction to the neglect of the other. According to Farber (1964:71), this depends on the nature of the specific interpersonal relationships involved. Turner (1969) notes that there are differences between husbands and wives in the extent to which one's own and one's spouse's kindred are seen. In summarizing the few existing studies of British kinship interaction, he suggests (1969:21) that husbands tend to strike a rough balance in maintaining social relations with their own and their wives's kindred, whereas the wife shows a bias toward maintaining more contacts with her own kindred.

Thus it can be seen that while the view that American kinship is composed of interlocking nuclear families is logical from a cultural standpoint, this perspective is inadequate to study the relational system of kinship. At this level the question of joint participation of spouses in kin affairs and equalitarian treatment of each kindred is an empirical one that involves the search for factors that may account for the imbalances which do occur across the marital pair. Not only do we lack sufficient information to account for imbalances in interaction with the kindred of each spouse, but there is also a paucity of information pertaining to social relations with in-marrying affines of focal ego's own kindred. However, some additional considerations may account for some of the differences which have been noted.

A major characteristic of our kinship system is the absence of any group of relatives outside the household. This means that, upon marriage, an individual does not retain a position in a more extended kin group and thus has more freedom to govern his affairs with kindred. This aspect of choice places the individual in a pivotal role with regard to maintaining or curtailing his contacts with his kindred—and each spouse in a marriage plays this pivotal role regarding relationships with his or her own kindred. Thus the necessary condition for one's spouse's kindred to be integrated into an individual's own network of relatives clearly depends on his spouse.

As Turner (1968:26) has suggested, it is realistic to assume that both the husband and the wife act as pivotal links in maintaining relationships with their respective kindred: if either the husband or wife is unable or unwilling to maintain social relationships with his or her kindred, then relationships with these kindred will be minimized for the conjugal pair. This suggests that the husband and wife provide the mediating link for their spouse in establishing and maintaining relationships with their own respective kindred.

However, it should be recognized that symmetry in the structure of the marital pair does not necessarily imply that spouses view their affines and consanguines as equally important. Although the ideal marital norms specify equalitarian treatment of the kindred of each spouse for interaction, one's social realtionships with one's own kindred may be more significant than relationships with inlaws. Schneider (1968:80, 92) notes that relationships with inlaws are not as binding as relationships with one's own kindred. Deaths, divorces, and remarriages of one's spouse raise additional problems with respect to an individual's relationships with these kin. The relative importance of affines and kindred is reflected in kinship reckoning. According to Schneider (1968:68), an individual's recognized kin are

... fundamentally consanguineal networks to which spouses are added. Inlaws are not common; in fact, they are notable by their absence. In genealogies, informants normally list their own spouse and the spouses of their blood relatives, but they do not often spontaneously list the parents or siblings of any of the spouses they list, and often not even the parents or siblings of their own spouse.

It follows from what has been said so far that if kindred ties have relatively greater significance than affinal ties, then an individual's relationship with in-marrying affines of his own bilateral kindred would be contingent on his relationship with a specific representative of his kindred. And his relationships with in-marrying affines of his spouse's kindred would depend on his spouse's relationship with specific representatives of her own kindred.

Thus by considering affines and consanguines this way, our model of the relational system of kinship can be modified. By taking an ego-centered approach, we make an individual's relationships with in-marrying affines of his own kindred contingent on his relationship with his kindred; and his relationships with his spouse's kindred's in-marrying affines contingent on his spouse's relationship with specific members of her kindred. What emerges, then, is not an "onion" structure of a series of interlocking nuclear families, but a *kindred-based model* of American kinship relations which is expanded by linkages to affines. The question of the extent to which these linkages are balanced is an empirical one—as is the determination of factors that lead to imbalances. But posing the problem of kinship in terms of such an ego-centered approach allows us to delineate factors that account for the differences among individuals in their relationships with affines as well as consanguines.

Kindred Types

In view of the foregoing discussion, and mindful that our study of kinship will examine the basis on which relatives are recruited for interaction, how shall we bring our general conception of a kindred-based model of kinship to the specific task of describing the concrete units of kinship manifest in patterns of interaction with relatives in the working class? A literal analysis of the role structure of an individual's universe of kin would involve separate treatment of ego's relationships with each relative occupying the kinship roles he recognized. Distinctions would be made among relatives in terms of genealogical distance and generational distance—whether the relative is in ego's direct line of descent or a direct descendant of ego's collaterals—as well as distinctions between ego's consanguines, his consanguines' affines, his spouse's consanguines, and their affines.

These distinctions are not usually used simultaneously in studies of American kinship structure and interaction for the good and sufficient reason that they are mindless categories by themselves. Depending on the problem focus, the number of categories is reduced by limiting the number of kinship roles considered, or by grouping categories of relatives on the basis of common kinship character-istics. Adams's study of urban kinship is an example. His analysis (1968:12) is based on relationships between respondents and three categories of their consanguineal kin: parents, siblings, and "secondary relatives." Secondary kin is a grouping of aunts, uncles, grandparents, cousins, and so on.

In the present study, the kin relationships investigated are limited to 30 distinct categories of relatives (see the questionnaire, Appendix A, questions number 152-162). Since the data gathered concern the respondent's contact with the complete pool of available kin, it is necessary to collapse these categories of relatives in order to identify salient characteristics of kin in a manner consistent with the views on kinship as a relational system spelled out in this chapter. For we wish to distinguish between ego's kindred and his spouse's kindred; ego's genealogically close kin and distant kin; and ego's ascendant and collateral kin as opposed to descendant kin. Thus the following criteria were employed to reduce the 30 terminologically distinct kinship roles for which data are available: First, the respondent's bilateral kindred and their in-marrying affines were differentiated from the respondent's spouse's bilateral kindred and their in-marrying affines. Second, genealogically close kin were distinguished from distant kin. And third, generation differences among the respondent's genealogically close kin were noted.

These distinctions collapse the 30 kinship roles into 4 types of kindred as follows. The first is termed the respondent's *spouse's kindred.* The relatives included in our enumeration who represent spouse's kindred are the spouse's kin of orientation. These are the respondent's spouse's parents and siblings. For our purposes the spouse's siblings' spouses are also included in what is termed spouse's kindred.

The remaining three categories comprise subtypes of the respondent's (as opposed to his or her spouse's) kindred. Thus what we shall term the respondent's genealogically *distant kindred* includes aunts, uncles, nephews, nieces, and grandparents. The respondent's genealogically close relatives include the kinship roles of the respondent's family of orientation and his family of procreation. In order to examine generational relationships, close kin of orientation are separated from close kin of procreation. Thus what we shall term the *close kindred* includes the roles of the respondent's parents and siblings. The respondent's siblings' spouses are also included in the category of close kindred. The respondent's *joint descendant kindred* includes kinship roles in his direct line of descent: respondent's children and their spouses, and the collective children of the foregoing.

This typology distinguishes ego's kindred and their in-marrying affines. Within ego's kindred, further distinctions are made by genealogical distance and generation. The typology preserves the meaning of the kindred as the consanguinal kin of the respondent or the respondent's spouse. However, the inclusion of in-marrying affines in the categories of relatives who we term kindred violates the strict etymological meaning of the concept. Turner (1968:19), for example, distinguishes ego's direct affines (i.e., spouse's kindred) from indirect affines (spouses of members of ego's kindred and spouses of members of ego's spouse's kindred) on the grounds that direct affines become the bilateral kin of ego's children while indirect affines do not.

The inclusion of in-marrying affines within types of kindred means that our typology is *kindred based* rather than a complete separation of ego's network of consanguines from his network of affines. If our research question merely asked whether kindred (blood) ties are stronger than kin ties by marriage (affines), there would be no justification for the inclusion of in-marrying affines in these categories. However, we wish to examine how other characteristics of kin are related to interaction as well. Either additional categories of kindred and nonkindred are required for the analysis or it is necessary to combine categories as we have just indicated. The former decision was rejected because it makes the analysis of the respondent's contacts with the complete pool of relatives exceedingly difficult.

Nevertheless, we encounter little loss in this decision. The question of whether kindred ties are stronger than affinal ties can be examined in this research. The categories referred to as spouse's kindred and close kindred are directly comparable in conceptualization, with the exception that spouse's kindred are the respondent's affines. Both categories are composed of the kinship roles of parents, siblings, and siblings' spouses. (A more literal analysis of this role structure will be made in Chapters 5 and 6 to examine the issue directly.)

It is crucial that the four types of kindred be recognized as categories of relatives and not as concrete groups. Relatives who comprise each category share common characteristics in terms of how they are related to ego. At this stage, the treatment of these four categories of kin and the distinction between the respondent's kindred and spouse's kindred must be considered a heuristic device that avoids the use of vague descriptive concepts such as "kin networks," and misleading concepts such as "extended family." (As we have noted, the assumptions underlying these latter concepts cannot be met by the knowledge that an individual has such relatives available to him or even that he contacts these kin.) At the same time, however, the kindred types conceptualized here permit us to discuss the complete pool of relatives, making distinctions along genealogical, generational, and consanguinal lines.

Design of the Research

The present study is descriptive and exploratory. It attempts to develop hypotheses about the bases upon which the geographically available pool of relatives is activated in terms of interaction, and thus to begin to explain the problem of variability in kinship behavior in western society. It relies on information about social contacts respondents had with relatives who lived within the same metropolitan area as themselves at the time of the interview. The period of contact is limited to the seven-day period preceding the interview.

The data on which this study is based concern ordinary daily contacts between our respondents and their relatives rather than crises, ceremonies, rituals, and so on, which allegedly bring kin together. This strategy was selected by choice because we wished to assess the social significance of kinship to our respondents, for it is in daily contact that the first basis for social relations occurs among kin, and it is the bulk of the total kin interaction that occurs.

These data were originally collected for a study of the role played by poverty and aging in the social isolation of the working class (Rosenberg, 1970). That initial analysis focused on a different problem from ours, devoted only a single chapter to kinship, and did not make the distinctions by type of kindred that are central to the present work. Hence this study is an extensive departure from the earlier one.

This study draws on a sample of 1,596 persons. They are white, working class people (and their spouses) between the ages of 45 and 79, who have held manual jobs all or most of their lives. The sample was restricted to a low income range: none were considered eligible unless the total yearly family income from all sources was less than $7,500.

The design of the original study required not only a sample of lower working class people in middle and old age, but also information about their neighbors. Accordingly, the following two-stage sample procedure was employed: The 13,754 blocks within the city limits of Philadelphia, Pennsylvania, were arrayed by census tract in a serpentine manner. A random number was drawn to designate the first block in the sample, and every thirty-fourth block thereafter was selected. In the second stage, a census of households was conducted in the blocks selected. It had a dual purpose of screening eligible respondents according to race, age, income, and occupational criteria of the study, and of describing the remaining ineligible respondents of the block. (This latter purpose is, of course, of no consequence for the present study.) On completion of screening, 230 of the 405 sample blocks were found to contain eligible respondents. Most of these were heads of households. If the spouse of the head of the household was living with the head at the time of the interview, the spouse was included in the sample regardless of age or employment status.

It should be understood that while the original study was designed to represent the substratum of the working class defined by the above-mentioned racial, occupational, income, and age characteristics, the present study does not aim at a specific population group. For this work has an exploratory and theoretical aim that logically requires a follow-up study on new populations for an understanding of the general scope of the findings—whether they are applicable in one class, for instance, or extend to all social ranks. However, it is also the case that the exploratory and theoretical aims of this study will press us in the concluding chapter to hypothesize concerning the wider applicability of our findings.

The field work was begun in March 1965, and was concluded at the end of May 1965. A staff of 50 professional interviewers, all with many years of interviewing experience, was assembled for this work. All the interviewers themselves fell within the age range of the respondents. Many of the interviewers, if not themselves working class people, were children of working class people; thus there was an inherent basis for rapport between interviewer and interviewee. There were only two interviewer resignations during the entire course of the field work.

Interviewers spent ten days in training for their task. A field manual was written for them specifically and was utilized throughout the training period. Pretests were conducted for the usual item estimation purposes and for insight into the interviewing problems which could be expected in the field. Linguistic barriers were eliminated by the employment of bilingual interviewers where required.

In view of the variability and optional nature of kin reckoning permitted by our kinship system, the decision was made not to rely on respondents reporting the existence of relatives. That is, those categories of relatives representing all possible primary and secondary kin were printed in the interview schedule; respondents were systematically questioned by the interviewer about people who occupied each kinship role.

Information was obtained from the respondents regarding the first name, age, residential location, and other characteristics of each relative. Additional information was obtained on social contacts with each relative the respondents reported as living within the Standard Metropolitan Statistical Area. For instance, respondents were asked the number of times in the past seven days they had had contacts with each relative reported in the metropolitan area. The question was worded: "How many times during the past seven days did you get together with (RELATIVE)?" (See Appendix A for questionnaire details.)

Plan of the Book

In elaborating our approach to kinship relations through data on kinship interaction in the working class, we will proceed as follows. In Chapter 2 we describe the availability of the relatives of our respondents in the Philadelphia

Standard Metropolitan Statistical Area. We pay special attention to the availability of each of the kindred types. In Chapter 3 we take account of the availability of kin and examine patterns of kinship interaction in terms of how many kindred types our respondents see and which specific kindred types are seen by most of them; how many relatives of each type are contacted; and how frequently. In this chapter we also examine the role played in kinship interaction by geographical distance from available relatives. The chief analytic focus of this chapter is the question of whether equalitarian norms or kinship norms play the predominant role in the relational system of kinship. In Chapter 4 we turn to the question of the persistence of patterns of kinship interaction throughout the life cycle. Here we examine age and marital status as life cycle indicators and attempt to clarify the role such factors play in contact with various kindred types.

In Chapter 5 we address the issue of matricentricity as a characteristic of kinship interaction in the working class by examining husband-wife differences in interaction with both close and spouse's kindred, and by ascertaining the effects of age and of conjugal role segregation on such differences. In Chapter 6 we expand considerably the focus of the preceding chapter and elaborate on consanguinal and affinal kinship relations as the central feature of the kindred-based linkage model of working class kinship, and more generally, of American kinship. In Chapter 7 we conclude this book with some interpretive and speculative observations on the significance of our approach to the relational system of kinship. In particular, we focus here on issues dealing with the relationship between the economy and kinship, and stratification and kinship. Appendix A contains the questionnaire.

Conclusion

In sum, this study is partly a reaction to the debate on the character of extra-familial kin ties in urban, industrial society. This debate has been cast in terms promoting confusion about normative and relational aspects of kinship. The concepts used to study kinship have also failed to account for the range of new facts to which they should be expected to apply. At no point in the literature has a viable model been proposed for the study of the social system of kinship interaction in our society.

Given these circumstances, it appears that a better general understanding can be gained by putting forth a model which at once fits the characteristics of the society and the complexities of the kinship system. After considering various lines of approach open to us, we arrived at the conclusion that the logical procedure to follow would be to devise a study with the primary aim of exploring the viability of the kindred. Thus we have proposed in this chapter what might be termed the kindred-based linkage model as a way of studying kinship. And we approach the elaboration of this model in the chapters below from the point of view of the empirical study of kinship interaction as reported by working class people.

The social significance of kinship depends on the extent to which it provides a basis for social relationships. While there is general recognition that the segment of a universe of kin who live in a contiguous area form an opportunity structure for purposes of interaction, nevertheless the questions of what factors are associated with the selection of kin from this pool of relatives, the extent to which this opportunity structure is utilized, and which of these relatives are seen, have not been thoroughly studied. Some individuals have a wider range of kin than others. The nature of these relationships differs for different individuals. Often the wife's relationship with her kindred is different from the husband's relationship with his kindred. Some relatives will be specifically excluded from some individuals' network of kin; others will be chosen for frequent interaction. What factors account for this variability? And how widespread is it?

The kindred-based linkage model provides us with a tool to begin to answer these questions. It points to the variability that is characteristic of the relational system and suggests that this variability can be understood by considering characteristics of the individual and his relatives, as well as by the nature of the kinship bond between them.

We need information about changes in an individual's socially effective kin as a consequence of age; the contexts in which one's own kindred, one's spouse's kindred, and in-marrying affines are seen equally and the contexts in which one or others are favored for interaction; and how the disruption of marriage is associated with interaction with one's own and one's spouse's kindred. Moreover, a major condition of rates of interaction is the extent to which the available opportunity structure of kinship is utilized. How are characteristics of the respondents and of their relatives associated with differential utilization of the local opportunity structure of kinship? Using an interaction criterion for kinship relations, a set of factors will be delineated which account for some of this variability.

This report must be seen as an attempt to develop a conceptually clear, empirical base for the substantiation and development of theory that explains the presence of ongoing relationships with kin living outside an individual's household. It approaches this task by attempting to account for the variability in these relationships. By proceeding in this manner we will show the viability of the kindred-based linkage model for the study of relational aspects of kinship in American society.

2

The Availability of Kin

Recent years have seen some advances in knowledge concerning the availability of kin. Studies indicate that individuals in urbanized, industrialized societies have a larger number of relatives geographically available to them than was previously thought. The contemporary urban dweller in the United States probably is the second or third generation of his family to reside in his city and has numerous relatives in the area. An intensive study of a small sample of working class couples (Komarovsky, 1962) also tends to support this hypthesis. And a recent review of the past ten years of work on this and related questions concludes, "proximity, not separation, is the rule, with actual geographical isolation from kin being characteristic of only a small portion of the population" (Adams, 1970: 578).

Whether urban man is more geographically separated from kin than people in preindustrial and industrializing societies remains an open question, however. According to Mirande (1969: 153-154), this issue can only be resolved with cross-cultural data. Yet Petersen (1969: 271), in a review of such data, concludes that we still do not know whether people in preindustrial and developing societies have more relatives available to them than people in urbanized, highly industrialized societies.

Within urbanized societies a great deal of variability has been found in the number of relatives different people have available to them. One factor said to be associated with this variability is social class: working class people having more relatives who are geographically available than middle class people. Yet, despite numerous studies of American kinship, we still lack an adequate description of the local kinship structure which goes beyond reporting the sheer number of relatives available.

Insufficiently detailed information about the role composition of the relatives available to an individual has prevented understanding the social relations that do develop among such kin. It has led to the use of misleading descriptive concepts, such as the extended family, as well as to lack of understanding of the bases on which choices are exercised in establishing social relationships with available kin. In fact much of the discussion of the alleged isolation of the urban dweller from his kin in industrialized societies lacks cogency because so few investigators account for limitations on, or opportunities for, interaction with kin afforded by the lesser or greater local availability of relatives. The term isolation has one meaning when relatives are not seen because most of them are far away, and another when they are not seen even though they live close by.

27

Moreover, even when accounting for the role of available kin as providing an opportunity structure, the issue is not simply one of how many relatives are recruited for interaction from the universe of kin. Of equal importance is the availability and differential recruitment of relatives by kinship relation: which kindred types are available, and among those available which are recruited? The meaning of isolation may depend on the social context of kindred types defined by geographical availability.

In this chapter, then, we examine the geographical availability of the relatives of our sample of urban, working class people in middle and old age. A description of the kinship structure available locally to these respondents will improve our understanding of the relation between the kinship system and the wider social structure. It will also tell a great deal about the extent to which kinship roles are filled on a locality basis. Insofar as local residence reinforces bonds of kinship (Mogey, 1964:516), these findings will point to the opportunities and limitations placed upon individuals in selecting among available kin for purposes of interaction. Such a description will also reveal the types of organization of kin which could potentially develop on a locality basis in order to perform socially relevant functions for these respondents, particularly if there is a grouping of kinship roles which is modal for the sample as a whole.

The Meaning of Propinquity

Numerous studies report on the geographical closeness of the kin of sampled respondents. The variability in the number of available kin reported by respondents in these studies and the lack of comparability of these findings present major problems in analysis and interpretation. Furthermore, there is some question as to what meaning can be attributed to studies reporting the number of kin available but not patterns of interaction among kin.

The lack of comparable findings is in part a result of differences in the method of enumerating kin and how geographical closeness or availability is measured. Differences in the number of kinship roles inquired about is a major problem. For example, Adams (1968:18) obtained his data by asking the respondent about his ascendant and collateral consanguines and their in-marrying affines who lived outside his household. He omitted all the respondent's descendants and the respondent's spouse's consanguinal kin and their affines. On the other hand, Reiss (1962:333) included kin up to first cousins. There are also differences in how geographical distance is measured. Some studies measure geographical distance by the number of miles an individual lives from relatives while others measure distance in terms of the number of hours it takes to get to a relative's home.

In addition to these differences, one must also consider the confounding effects of whether: (1) the unit of analysis is an individual (Cumming and

Schneider, 1961) or the domestic unit (Winch, Greer, and Blumberg, 1967), and whether (2) the interviewee is acting as a respondent (Adams, 1968) who reports on the kin enumerated on a questionnaire or interview or as an informant (Homans and Schneider, 1955) who reports on relatives he recognizes.

The variability in the number of kin reported by respondents is also related to the way bilateral kinship systems operate. If one were to trace out an individual's universe of kin in the bilateral system with any degree of thoroughness, an exceedingly large and meaningless number of kin roles would be found to be occupied by living people in each generation. It is a matter of ethnographic record that societies have found ways to reduce this number of relatives and consequently reduce the number of relatives with whom social relationships may develop. For example, Mogey (1964:507) reports reliance on endogamy, in particular a preference for a double collateral bond at marriage, to reduce this number of relatives. In this situation, brothers may marry their first cousins with the result that children of these unions share grandparents. Schneider (1968:69) suggests that one way the number of recognized kin is reduced in our society is by not tracing ascendents very far, thus avoiding the inclusion of more distant collaterals. Furthermore, in our society a large proportion of the culturally defined relatives of some remove are not recognized by individuals as kin. This is also a consequence of our kinship system. The relatively nonobligatory nature of this system means than an individual may choose whether or not to recognize some people as relatives.

However, once the universe of recognized kin is accurately described there arises the equally important problem of what meaning to ascribe to the pool of geographically available relatives. While research (Adams, 1968; Reiss, 1962; Sussman, 1965) on kin relations in the United States consistently demonstrates that increasing geographical distance of an individual from his relatives' residences limits his contact with them, the social significance of the relatives available locally also clearly depends upon the extent to which the system of kinship provides a basis for social interaction. Any interpretation of the meaning of the local kinship structure in terms of social interaction therefore must conform with characteristics of bilateral kinship systems and, in our society, the structural differentiation of this system from other societal systems.

Partly because the most stringent economic obligations to kin in our society occur within the domestic unit, and partly because of the nonobligatory meaning of kinship in bilateral systems, an individual is given some as yet unknown degree of latitude in deciding whether he has any duties toward available kin who do not reside in the same household, and in selecting them for interaction. Geographically available kin are not necessarily a concrete kin group or a network of relatives. Because an individual has relatives in an area, it neither follows from the nature of our kinship system that they will all be seen, nor that he or they established proximate residence because of kinship.

The fact that a meaningful social relationship is not obligatory upon all who are kin is an important characteristic of our kinship system and of bilateral systems generally. Strictly speaking, geographically available relatives are people who are defined as relatives by our kinship system and who, for various reasons, live within a circumscribed geographical area. They are relatives by virtue of ascription by the cultural system only. Such kin therefore constitute a source of potential social relationships. They are relatives with whom (perhaps because they live nearby) one may enter into continued or sustained interaction, and who may be, but not necessarily are, important in one's daily life.

Any attempt to circumscribe a geographical area that defines a relative as "available" is somewhat arbitrary. The criterion employed in this study is to consider as available only those relatives who could be visited or telephoned with relatively little cost to the respondent in time or expense. The boundaries of the Philadelphia Standard Metropolitan Statistical Area (SMSA) served this purpose, reflecting a somewhat coordinated transportation and communication system. Relatives considered geographically available are those who lived within this area at the time of the interview.

The Availability of Kindred Types

The size and composition of an individual's pool of available relatives is the consequence of complex social processes. It varies among different individuals and for each individual it changes over time. Such variability, while partly due to the vicissitudes of biological reproduction, might also be expected in a society where residence is defined as neolocal, and where the kinship system lacks principles necessary for forming major kin groups outside the domestic unit. Thus a multiplicity of factors is involved in the dispersion of kin. For example, the specific relatives an individual has available to him in a local area is a reflection of his migrations, and also of his relatives' migrations. Among factors associated with the respondent, some impinge directly on the size and composition of his available set of kin. Here research has found that length of residence is important. Other factors, associated with an individual's stage in the life cycle, impinge indirectly on the respondent's pool of relatives. Of these, age and marital status are important. They affect the role composition of an individual's universe of living relatives, and in this way are associated with which relatives are available.

From the point of view discussed in the preceding chapter, it is crucial to know the extent to which different types of kinship roles are reported together in the local area by the same individual. What is the nature of the actual—as opposed to the theoretical—opportunity structure of kinship roles occupied on a local basis? Do respondents have a variety of kinship roles from which to select for interaction, or is their selection limited by the availability of particular types of relatives?

In the preceding chapter we discussed the way the complexities of the role structure of the respondent's universe of kin could be simplified for this analysis by use of a kindred typology that identifies particular kinship roles, yet allows us to describe the composition of the complete pool of relatives available to respondents in a manner which is consistent with certain theoretical considerations of American kinship. Here we will first describe the size of our respondent's pool of available relatives: that is, those relatives who lived within the Philadelphia SMSA. Second, and more important, we shall provide detailed information about the role composition—in terms of kindred types—of the relatives who constitute the respondent's pool of available kin. In this way we will be able to evaluate the opportunities and limitations placed upon individuals in selecting among available kin for interaction.

The 1,596 working class people in middle and old age who comprised our total sample reported 23,580 people living outside their households who occupied the kinship roles enumerated on the questionnaire. Of these relatives 15,695 (or 66 percent) lived within the Philadelphia SMSA at the time of the interview. This figure—indicating that two-thirds of all relatives reside in the same metropolitan area as the respondents—is somewhat higher than reports from other studies. Reiss (1962:335—336) states that approximately 49 percent of his middle class Bostonians' relatives lived within the same metropolitan area as his respondents. Adams (1968:22) reports that 48 percent of his respondents' relatives lived within a one hundred mile radius of Greensboro, North Carolina. However, he found that his working class respondents reported more of their relatives within a 100-mile area than his middle class respondents. Not only are there class differences in these studies, but also differences in the ages of the samples. The respondents of Reiss and Adams are younger than the respondents who make up this study; furthermore, there are differences in the kin enumerated in these studies.

The 15,695 kin who were reported as available to our working class sample are related to 90 percent (1,434) of the respondents. Of the remaining 10 percent, or 162 respondents, 36 had no living kin whatever, 126 had relatives living beyond the SMSA only, and two respondents had relatives in the area who were not listed in the questionnaire. The 1,434 respondents who reported 15,695 geographically available kin possess a mean of 11.13 kin per respondent within the SMSA, and a standard deviation of 8.76. Kin available in the Philadelphia SMSA ranged from 1 to 54 relatives per respondent, with the sample skewed to the lower end of this range: 90 percent of the 1,434 respondents reported from 1 to 22 geographically available relatives. The median number of kin in the area is 8.10.

The variability in the size of available pools of relatives of these respondents reflects the complexity of factors associated with geographical dispersion and propinquity that occur among kin. The fact that most of the respondents report relatives available to them, and that these relatives are a fairly large proportion of the total number reported living, simply means that the respondents know of people who are ascribed the status of relative on the basis of our kinship system and that these relatives live within the same metropolitan area. Nothing is implied about which kinship roles are occupied on a locality basis or the role composition of this pool of kin. These relatives represent different degrees of genealogical and generational remove.

In the remainder of this chapter we are concerned with this issue: the composition of the available pool of relatives. We will limit our discussion to those 1,434 respondents with kin living outside their household but within the metropolitan area. The role composition of these pools of kin will be examined in terms of the four kindred types.

Two dimensions pertaining to the role composition of an individual's pool of kin are important in the present context. First is the number of different kindred types the respondents report in the area, which will indicate in a general way the variety of available relatives from among whom he could choose for interaction. Second is the actual role composition of this pool of kin, shown by the presence of various combinations of the four types of kindred. Here we will find whether any particular combination of available kindred types might characterize the sample as a whole and whether particular kindred types tend to be reported together.

The number of kindred types reported within the metropolitan area by these respondents is shown in Table 2-1. The majority of this sample of working class people do not report a full complement of kinship roles available to them. Only about 12 percent reported all four kindreds in their pool of available relatives in the Philadelphia SMSA—that is, at least one representative of each of the four kindred types was available to only 169 of our respondents. The remaining 1,265 respondents who reported fewer than four kindred types are approximately equally distributed in reporting one, two, and three types of kindred available in their local pool of relatives. And about 60 percent reported representatives of only one or two kindred types available to them.

Whatever else is said in the remainder of this chapter about the composition of our sample's universe of kin, the overriding fact of kinship for these working class people is that the available pool of kin is markedly incomplete. In all but

Table 2-1
Respondents with Various Numbers of Kindred Types Available in the Philadelphia SMSA (In Percentages)

	One Kindred Type	Two Kindred Types	Three Kindred Types	Four Kindred Types	Total
	28.2%	32.1%	27.9%	11.8%	100%
	(404)	(460)	(401)	(169)	(1,434)

12 percent of the cases, our respondents are limited in selecting kin for interaction because, for any given individual, numerous kinship roles are unavailable. The next question, then, is which kindred types are available or unavailable? And in particular, does the lack of completeness negate the possibility that representatives of certain crucial sets of kinship roles can be recruited for interaction—specifically, kin stemming from the so-called nuclear family and kin who represent the bilateral kindred.

In this working class sample, the largest proportion of people have representatives of close kindred available to them. Close kindred were reported in the pool of relatives of 65 percent (934 persons) of the respondents. Sixty percent (857 persons) of the respondents reported distant kindred within the metropolitan area. Fifty-four percent (781 persons) reported representatives of joint descendant kindred living within the metropolitan area. And representatives of spouse's kindred were available to only 44 percent (631 persons) of the respondents.

It is evident that few respondents lacked representatives of nuclear family kinship roles among their pool of available relatives. These roles (parents, siblings, children) are found with their affines in the close and joint descendant kindred. (That is, close kindred are kin of orientation with in-marrying affines and joint descendants are their collective children with in-marrying affines.) For only ten percent of the sample (144 persons) are neither close nor joint descendant kindred represented in the pool of available kin.

However, an incompleteness should be noted. Of the 1,434 respondents who did report representatives of these kindred stemming from their nuclear family, only about 30 percent (425 persons) reported representatives of both close *and* joint descendant kindred. These 425 persons comprise about 41 percent of those with two or more kindred types available to them. Thus the opportunity exists for a majority of the respondents to have contact with some primary kin—that is, genealogically close kin who at some time in the respondent's life cycle were likely to have lived in the same household. Yet at the same time the interlocking of two generations of nuclear units, represented chiefly by siblings and children, is impossible within the compass of available kin for all but a third of these working class people. The intergenerational connection between nuclear units is fragmented by the lack of availability of members, and this interlocked set of kin cannot therefore be a unit of kinship interaction for the majority of these working class people.

Very few respondents reported no representatives whatsoever of their bilateral kindred among their pool of relatives. The bilateral kindred (and these relatives' affines) are included in the distant, close, and joint descendant types of kindred. Four percent of the sample (40 persons) did not have representatives of at least one of these sub-types—that is, they had only representatives of spouse's kindred—in their pool of relatives. However, as is the case with nuclear family roles, completeness is relatively rare. A complete bilateral kindred simply is not available to most respondents. Only about 20 percent of the sample (290 persons) reported representatives of the three kindred types comprising their bilateral kindred (close, distant, and joint descendants) among their pool of relatives. These 290 respondents represent 51 percent of the 570 persons with three or more types of kindred in their pool of relatives. Since a complete bilateral kindred is not likely to be available, the three kindred types comprising the bilateral kindred could not be a unit of kinship interaction for most of these working class respondents. That is to say, only fragmented bilateral kindred is available to most respondents.

We previously noted that 44 percent of the respondents reported representatives of their spouse's kindred available to them. However, our enumeration of kin did include more kinship roles in ego's own kindred than in his spouse's kindred. For example, the enumeration did not include the respondent's spouse's distantly related kin, while it did include the respondent's own distantly related kin. The kinship roles comprising spouse's kindred are the respondent's spouse's kin of orientation and their in-marrying affines. As a kindred type, its composition is comparable to the respondent's close kindred. As close kindred and spouse's kindred are purportedly treated equally for purposes of interaction, the question arises, To what extent are both these types of kindred available to the respondents? Is asymmetry in interaction a function of opportunity structure or a counter-normative pattern?

Thirty percent of the total sample of respondents (430 persons) reported both close and spouse's kindred in their pool of relatives. These 430 respondents represent about 42 percent of those respondents with two or more types of kindred in their pool of relatives. Thus, less than a third of the total sample of 1,434 respondents with kin the SMSA have the choice of seeing either or both of their own close kindred and their spouse's close kindred. Obviously, the overwhelming majority of working class people sampled here are not able to comply with equalitarian kinship norms and thus a major share of observed asymmetry in interaction must be due to the opportunity structure.

Of all the possible permutations and combinations of kindred, the two kindred types that are reported together by the largest number of respondents are close and distant. Forty-five percent of the sample (642 respondents) reported representatives of close and distant kindred among their pool of relatives. (These respondents represent 62 percent of those respondents with two or more types of kindred available to them.) This pattern is also reflected among respondents with exactly two types of kindred in their pool of relatives, where we find the highest proportion (38.5 percent) reporting close and distant kindred available to them. In addition, few respondents do not report representatives of distant kindred in their pool of relatives *without* also reporting close kindred. Thus, of the 857 respondents reporting representatives of distant kindred, about 75 percent (642 people) also reported close kindred in their pool of relatives. However, more respondents reported close kindred without also reporting distant kindred. Of the 934 respondents with close kindred available to them, 68 percent also reported distant kindred. Thus, while few respondents do not report representatives of distant kindred without close kindred, representatives of close kindred are more likely to be reported separately. In fact, twice as many respondents with only one type of kindred in the area report close rather than distant kindred.

In order to explain why respondents report representatives of their distant kindred along with representatives of their close kindred, we must look more closely at the role composition of these two types of kindred. Ninety-five percent of the relatives who comprise *close kindred* in the metropolitan area are the respondent's siblings and siblings' spouses.[a] Eighty-eight percent of the kinship roles comprising available distant kindred are ego's sibling's children, i.e., the respondent's nephews and neices, The remaining 12 percent are grandparents, aunts, and uncles. It is likely that when the respondent reports both close and distant kindred in his pool of relatives, he is often reporting his siblings *and* his siblings' children. The question arises whether or not the association between reporting close and distant kindred together occurs because representatives of these two types of kindred are housed together in the same domestic unit. We cannot answer this question directly, as we do not have information on the composition of the households of the relatives who were reported. However, we have indirect information which does bear on this issue, namely the ages of the sibling's children. Over 70 percent of the respondents' siblings' children are over 25 years of age.

If age is any reflection of whether or not siblings' children are housed with the respondent's siblings—and we believe it is a fairly accurate one—then the association between reporting representatives of close and distant kindred is not entirely due to these kin being housed together. Hence, while we do not have the data directly supporting our view, we feel confident that a large proportion of the approximately 45 percent of the respondents who reported both distant and close kindred among their pool of relatives did so because of the tendency of adult children—in this case siblings' children—to live in the same metropolitan area as their parents. In this case the parents are the respondent's siblings. The tendency for adult children to live near their parents is also reflected in the fact that 54 percent of the sample of respondents reported joint descendant kindred in the metropolitan area.

Turning to the composition of the entire sample's total pool of available relatives, we find a highly scattered patterning of the possible permutations of various kindred types. Every one of the 15 permutations logically possible by combining the four kindred types exists for some respondents, but no one combination is markedly modal in this working class sample. However, the distributions across all types of kindred is not random. Table 2-2 presents the

---

[a]The remaining five percent are parents of the respondent. The small number of parents reported in the metropolitan area reflects the age of our sample. Actually, 75 percent of all living parents resided within the metropolitan area.

Table 2-2
Respondents Reporting Various Permutations of Kindred Types
in the Philadelphia SMSA, in Rank Order
(In Percentages and Cumulative Percentages)

Kindred Type	Percent of Respondents	Cumulative Percents
Only joint descendant kindred	13.8	13.8
Close and distant kindred	12.3	26.1
Close, distant and spouse's kindred	12.2	38.3
Close, distant, spouse's and joint descendants	11.8	50.1
Close, distant, and joint descendant kindred	8.4	58.5
One close kindred	8.0	66.5
Close and joint descendant kindred	6.3	72.8
Joint descendant, distant and spouse's kindred	4.3	77.1
Distant and spouse's kindred	3.7	80.8
Only distant kindred	3.6	84.4
Joint descendant and distant kindred	3.5	87.9
Joint descendent and spouse's kindred	3.3	91.2
Joint descendant, close and spouse's kindred	3.1	94.3
Close and spouse's kindred	2.9	97.2
Only spouse's kindred	2.7	99.9
Total	(100.0)	(100.0)

proportion of respondents reporting each of the fifteen combinations of kindred types, ranked in descending order and with cumulative percentages. Of the fifteen possible permutations of kindred types by which a pool of relatives could be constituted, seven account for the actual composition of the pool of kin of about 73 percent of the respondents.

The largest number of respondents reported only representatives of their joint descendant kindred in their pool of relatives. These respondents represent 49 percent of those with one type of kindred available to them and about fourteen percent of the total sample of respondents. This finding is reflected in the results of other studies (e.g., Adams, 1968) that report the tendency of adult children of working class people to live near their parents. Not only is this true for our respondents, but those of our respondents who have only joint descendant kindred available are the modal type in terms of all possible permutations of relatives a person may possess. In addition, among the seven highest ranking combinations, either close or joint descendant kindred (nuclear family roles) are included in each case. Furthermore, it should be noted that while the full complement of types of kindred is available to only about 12 percent of the sample, this particular permutation of available kindred ranks fourth highest among all possible permutations for the sample as a whole.

What does stand out is the fact that no one combination of types of available kindred is characteristic of this sample. Rather, there is great variability in the extent to which different kinship roles are filled on a locality basis, and thus in which combinations of the four types of kindred are available to our respondents as a basis for social interaction. One or a few types of kindred do not appear to be overwhelmingly represented in most of the pools of kin for this section of the working class.

Conclusion

In this chapter we have examined the availability of relatives of our urban sample of middle aged and old working class Philadelphians. Relatives who live within a contiguous geographical area have been viewed as a pool of kin from which an individual may select for interaction. Our major concern has been with the composition of this pool of relatives in terms of kindred types. We have obtained a detailed description of the local opportunity structure of kinship roles that exists in a typical metropolis for respondents of designated age and class level; and we have laid the groundwork for a careful evaluation, in the next chapter, of interaction that occurs among available kin plus the extent to which the availability of certain types of kindred provide a basis for such contact.

A great deal of variability has been found in the composition of different individuals' pools of kin. But whether or not one may conclude that these working class people have a variety of kinship roles represented in their pools of relatives from which they may recruit kin for interaction clearly depends on the criterion used. Except for the minority of 28 percent of our sample, who reported representatives of only one type of kindred in the metropolitan area, our findings document the view that working class people have some choices in selecting from among broad categories of kinship roles for interaction. Such choices, however, are not unlimited. Only 12 percent of the sample reported the full complement of four kindred types among their pool of relatives; and the pools of relatives available to most respondents lack representatives of numerous kinship roles.

Not only are these respondents, then, limited in the opportunities they have in selecting kin for interaction, but the actual composition of their pool of relatives is variable. No one combination of the four types of kindred is clearly modal for the sample; and each of the fifteen logically possible combinations of the four types is reported by some respondents.

The role composition of the pool of relatives for this sample is best characterized as an indistinct structure. Not only do few respondents have all four types of kindred represented within the area, but few have the opportunity to choose for interaction from among the three types comprising their bilateral kindred. Moreover, only a fragment of the possible roles represented in the three bilateral kindred types are available to most respondents. However, in support of the findings of other studies, there is the tendency of adult children to reside within the same area as their parents. This is reflected by the number of respondents who report joint descendant kindred available, as well as the pattern of distant and close kindred reported by the same respondents.

We do not know whether the composition of our urban sample and the sample members' pool of relatives is similar to what would be found in other less urbanized, less industrialized societies with bilateral kinship systems. The data we have presented do not contradict Greenfield's thesis (1961:312) that the fragmented kindred is present in the same form in industrialized, urbanized societies and in societies where industrialization and urbanization have not occurred. We feel that the variablity found in the types of kindred that are available is a consequence of the absence in our society of residence rules that favor aggregates of particular kin living near one another, and the absence in our kinship system of descent principles that might favor the grouping of specific kin. In fact, even if each respondent were to have close, meaningful relationships with each of the kin available to him, the result would nevertheless be an indistinct pattern of interaction given the limited categories of relatives available. However, we will defer until the next chapter discussion of whether any distinct groupings of kindred types emerges from these indistinct opportunity structures when interaction with kin does occur.

Also, lacking a middle class sample, we do not know whether the composition of these working class respondents' pools of relatives are class specific. Since some studies (Adams, 1968; Mirande, 1969) have presented evidence indicating that working class people have larger numbers of relatives available to them than more geographically mobile middle class people, one might expect that the composition of the pool of relatives locally available for middle class people would be more variable and indistinct in terms of opportunity structure.

The question arises whether or not our data indicate the presence of kinship roles that could comprise what in any sense of the term might be referred to as an extended family. The answer to this question depends again on the criterion utilized. As noted in the preceding chapter, the presence of a functioning extended family, in terms of the precise meaning of the concept, is uncommon in bilateral kinship systems (Murdock, 1968), and rare in societies where the economy is based on wage labor (Greenfield, 1961).[b] However, sociologists do not define the concept rigorously. According to Sussman (1968:126), in a usage with which we disagree, the structure identified as the modified extended family is composed of nuclear families. Thus, the concept is in this way used to refer to relations between kin-related domestic units. On this ground, clearly each of the 1,434 respondents with relatives living outside their households but within the metropolitan area has the opportunity to establish relationships with at least one such domestic unit.

In our opinion, however, the issue is not the presence of households with relatives in the area, but the presence of (and interaction with) different types and members of kindred, as we have argued in Chapter 1. In that chapter, we argued that the presence of various kindred types cannot be conceived as a measure of the extended family. And indeed, we have seen in this chapter that however we think of kin-related domestic units—whether as interlocking nuclear families or modified extended families or bilateral kindred—there is the possibility of only 20 to 30 percent of these working class people recruiting from a complete roster of members of such kinship formations through interaction. The opportunity structure will support no greater proportion.

One study of urban kinship has presented a more sensitive measure of "extended familism" (or fragmentation of localized kinship structure) than whether any relatives outside the household are available. Here it will be instructive to compare the extent of fragmentation of our sample's pools of relatives with that sample's pool of available kin. Winch et al. (1967:265-272), in a study of middle class kinship relations, created a measure of the extent to which different kinship roles were available, a measure which he termed "intensity of presence." Although much looser than our kindred type of classification, the intensity of presence index is similar to a regrouping of combinations of kindred types and thus permits a comparison with our data. Since their sample is limited to married respondents, the findings we present for comparison are limited to the married people in our study. Winch et al. defined intensity of presence by the extent to which different *households* of the respondent's close consanguines (i.e., close and/or joint descendant kindred), spouse's close kin (i.e., spouse's kindred), and more distant kin (i.e., distant kindred) were represented in the metropolitan area of Chicago (1967:267).

The localized kinship structure of the pool of relatives for their middle class sample is as indistinct as our own. For 37 percent of the married, middle class sample Winch studied, representatives of close or joint, spouses', and distant kin were available. The comparable figure in the present study for our married

---

[b]Zelditch (1964:468) makes the additional point that an extended family can be created by any residence rule *other* than that of neolocal. Our residence rules are, of course, neolocal. In an extended family, the core of the members remaining in their natal homes are linked by descent. It is a group of relatives greater than the nuclear family living together and subordinated to the same authority.

respondents is about 32 percent. While these two studies sample different socioeconomic levels, there is no indication on the basis of the evidence that there are differences by class in the extent to which different kinship roles are represented within the metropolitan areas.

The findings presented in this chapter indicate that variability, indistinctness, and fragmentation are appropriate terms to characterize the role structure of this working class sample's pools of available relatives. However, mere knowledge of a relative living within a contiguous area does not necessarily mean that he will be seen. What is important is the extent to which this opportunity structure of available kinship roles is utilized and whether it becomes functionally more distinct through selective utilization. The question of the extent to which available relatives are seen, and the bearing of the local opportunity structure of types of kindred on such interaction, is the matter to which we turn in the next chapter.

3

Kinship Interaction and the Local Opportunity Structure

To understand the relational system of kinship it is necessary to know how much interaction among kin depends on the rights and obligations people incur through ties of blood and marriage and how much it depends on other factors. The prime obstacle to this understanding is the dispersion of relatives beyond a geographical area where they are conveniently available for social relations. As the preceding chapter has made clear, relatively few people have no choice among categories of kin of partners for interaction; but also relatively few have available the full complement of kindred types from which to choose for social relations. For the bulk of these working class people, then, interaction with their relatives occurs in a context of limited choice—moderately or severely limited depending on the number of kindred types available. And the composition as well as the size of the available set of kindred types varies from person to person.

Given these sources of variability in size and composition of the opportunity structure of available kin, it becomes even more imperative to know what consistency, if any, exists in the bases of recruitment of kin for interaction. However, even if the kin of these working class people were not widely dispersed, the question of the extent to which interaction depended on ties of blood or marriage would still have to be raised. And even if all living relatives were geographically close, it is extremely unlikely that people would sustain social relationships with all their recognized kin. How, then, might they choose among them? Under these conditions of optimal availability of relatives, the question of the criteria by which relatives are selected for interaction would remain relevant.

In approaching this question we will examine characteristics of the respondents' relatives as well as characteristics of the respondents themselves. As we have implied earlier, both are associated with whether specific relatives are seen. In this chapter we will analyze the aspect of the problem dealing with characteristics of our respondents' relatives: how is the local opportunity structure of kinship associated with variability in kinship behavior? Inferences made from this information will throw light on the principle by which kin are selected for interaction. In Chapter 4 we will look more closely at characteristics of our respondents themselves.

Equalitarian Norms and Kinship Interaction

There is nearly universal agreement on the proposition that the mere knowledge of a relative living in a contiguous area does not mean that he will be contacted.

41

However, debate revolves around the criteria of selection and the importance of various factors in the selection process. The major alternative advanced to the selection of kin for interaction on the basis of considerations of consanguinity and genealogical distance is what might be termed the principle of equalitarianism. Establishing or maintaining social relations with kin living outside the household is said not to depend on the deference owed one kinsman by another. Obligations of kinship do not extend to sociability, presumably because of the differentiation of kinship from other institutional areas (especially the economy) in industrialized societies. Thus, Mogey (1964:506) and Cumming and Schneider (1961:501) suggest that a primary basis for recruitment of relatives in our society lies in socioemotional attitudes. From the point of view of these authors, there is socioemotional equality among kin such that regardless of the kinship relation between two people, relatives who live outside an individual's household but within a contiguous area are treated equally for purposes of interaction.

Both Mogey and Cumming and Schneider come to these conclusions from somewhat different perspectives and they do not provide data on interaction to support their claims. Both attempt to provide an orientation to social relationships that occur among kin in terms of the articulation of the kinship system and the society. Since bilateral kinship systems accumulate large numbers of kin in each generation, Mogey (1964:506-507) correctly points out that it would be impossible for an individual to fulfill obligations to a large proportion of his recognized kin. We noted in Chapter 1 that a consequence of this accumulation of relatives is that few individuals in our society even know the names of people who occupy all the kinship roles they recognize. Examining cross-cultural data, Mogey (1964:504) finds that structural arrangements in societies with bilateral kinship systems reduce potential social relations with kin by (1) endogamy—a preferential marriage system with one's own consanguinal kin; (2) disregarding genealogical depth in recognition—here grandparents are rarely known; and (3) establishing relationships with those relatives who are geographically available and selecting among these kin on the basis of nonkinship attributes related to compatibility. Hence socioemotional equality.

Cumming and Schneider pose the issue in a different manner but come to the same general conclusions. They examine how certain values in our society bear upon which relatives are socioemotionally close to an individual and therefore which would be favored for interaction. Given the broad institutional setting of American kinship and given our equalitarian values, recruitment of kin must comport with the norm of free choice. Cumming and Schneider argue that no particular type of kinship role is necessarily favored for interaction and there are no set modes of deference between generations. For example, some parents were omitted from what their respondents considered as intimate kin, and others gave the same status to a sibling or cousin as to their own children. Cumming and Schneider (1961:506) contrast their findings with Firth's (1956) results in his study of British kinship in London, where intimacy was directly related to closeness of consanguinity. According to Cumming and Schneider (1961:501), "There appears to be a selection of people who live nearby on the grounds of personal compatibility."

Mogey and Cumming and Schneider thus imply that considerations of genealogical distance and consanguinity are not as important in determining which relatives are seen as are nonkinship factors such as characteristics of the relative's status set and where the relative lives. They are pointing to the weakness of the kinship system that permits variability in patterns of recruitment. In fact, Cumming and Schneider are interested in the substitution of particular kinship roles by other kinship roles and by friends. From their perspective, the weakness of the kinship system, that is the absence of binding obligations to kin living outside the household, permits an individual to shift intense relationships from one type of relative—e.g., adult children—to another, such as siblings, as he moves through the life cycle, or as it fits his whim, need, or special interest.

Existing evidence suggests that the equalitarian thesis characteristic of the perspective of Mogey and Cumming and Schneider requires some modification. Moreover, this evidence raises questions regarding how the thesis of a socio-emotionally equalitarian kinship emphasis should be reformulated. In a number of studies examining respondents' contacts with available representatives of their own bilateral kindred, the norm of equalitarianism or free choice does not appear to operate in the relational system of kinship. These studies consistently demonstrate that people do not treat geographically available kindred equally for interaction but rather make distinctions among them primarily on the basis of genealogical considerations.

According to Sussman (1965:92) the relationships between adult children and their parents is the most important kinship bond in our society as evidenced by patterns of contact, aid, help, and support. Adams (1968:17) found that considerations of genealogical closeness among kindred was a primary basis upon which his middle and working class Greensboro respondents chose which kin they considered as intimates. In particular he found that parents and siblings were more likely to be seen than aunts, uncles, and cousins. And, using a monthly contact score, Reiss (1962:336) found that a higher proportion of his middle class respondents' available (i.e., in the same metropolitan area—Boston) parents and siblings were seen than more distantly related kindred.

While this discussion has been confined to an individual's relationships with relatives who comprise his own bilateral kindred, this should not be taken to mean that affines have been excluded from consideration in the controversy over equalitarianism. The equalitarian thesis has also been extended to include recruitment of spouse's kindred. Komarovsky states (1962:254) that there is a normative pattern of treating relatives comprising one's own bilateral kindred and the kindred of one's spouse equally for interaction. This particular aspect of the equalitarianism question will be examined in detail in Chapter 5.

Those who take the position that the principle of selectivity underlying the recruitment of kin for interaction is equalitarianism do not thereby rest the entire weight of explanation for kinship interaction on the personal likes or needs of relatives. The thesis of an equalitarian kinship emphasis does not rule out all other factors but socioemotional closeness. Relations with kin, these writers claim, can also be affected by factors which are themselves extraneous to kinship, or are related to the system of kinship but not a constituent part of it. In this view it is precisely the lack of relational norms specifically based on kinship which not only permits wide latitude in behavior among kin, but also allows the intrusion of nonkinship factors which themselves may explain some variability in contact. Several such factors have been adduced. The one germane to the present argument is related to the local opportunity structure of kinship—geographical distance.

Considered as a dimension of the local opportunity structure, the issue we are concerned with here is what meaning may be attributed to an association between geographical distance among kin and interaction. Certainly consensus exists that geographical distance between an individual and his relatives places constraints on the kinds and amounts of interaction that can occur with those who live at a distance. But the crux of the matter, for present purposes, would seem to lie elsewhere. Are kin ties disrupted by the dispersion of relatives, and, more importantly, does geographical distance differentially affect interaction with particular categories of relatives? Mogey and Cumming and Schneider take these issues to the extreme of the equalitarian position. They suggest that regardless of the specific kin relation between individuals, geographical distance has an attenuating effect on contact. Reiss's study supports this perspective. He found (1962:335) that the residential variable had a closer relationship to the number of kin seen than did degree of kin relation. However, Reiss's categories of geographical distance were broadly conceived—ranging from the city of Boston to the eastern United States.

But on the whole, studies of the social relationships which occur among kin have not done justice to the issues implicit in the perspective of Mogey and Cumming and Schneider. No one has examined, for instance, the relationship between the availability (or lack of it) of specific categories of kin and variation in interaction with relatives in certain kinship roles. And thus, for example, we cannot tell whether or to what extent more distantly related kin are seen as substitutes for more closely related kin who are unavailable. Moreover, such studies have not refined the notion of availability of kin to the point of considering the complex interrelations of degrees of residential proximity and kinship role among those relatives who live in the same metropolitan area. As a result, we do not know how the presence of a given type of kin in an individual's immediate vicinity affects his interaction with the same type of relative who lives farther away, but still within the metropolitan area.

In view of the evidence which presently can be brought to bear on this entire question of kinship norms versus equalitarian norms as criteria of selection of kin for interaction, and on the related questions of availability and geographical distance of kin, there are no compelling reasons for espousing either of these alternatives to the exclusion of the other. There are attractive aspects of the Mogey-Cumming and Schneider-Komarovsky position as well as of the Sussman-Adams-Reiss perspective. Dilemmas such as this usually indicate that both parties to the controversy are contributing valid elements to the overall picture, but that we need a more thorough understanding of the relationship of these elements to each other. When we examine the joint effects of kinship relation and opportunity structure on interaction we will have a better picture of this relationship.

Before doing so, however, one other general feature of the relational system of kinship ought to be noted. It too is the subject of controversy, and concerns the quality of the relationships that do occur among kin. Mogey (1964:507) characterizes relationships with relatives living outside an individual's household as sporadic rather than regular; voluntary rather than obligatory. Now it is true that our society does not have the structural supports for obligatory relationships among kin not living in the same household. Nevertheless a number of investigators have questioned (albeit indirectly) on the basis of research evidence, whether social relationships that do occur among kin are voluntary, and the extent to which they are sporadic. These researchers generally refer to the perceived importance of relatives among various populations. Greer (1956), for example, found that visiting among relatives was one of the most important primary group activities for his urban sample. Similarly, Axelrod and Sharp (1956) reported that residents of Detroit were more likely to participate socially with relatives than with neighbors or friends. Dotson (1951) found that visiting among relatives was very important for his working class sample. And, of course, the views of Sussman (1962) and Litwak (1960) rest on the assumption that kinship relations are something more than sporadic and voluntary. While these findings are hardly conclusive evidence, they do seem to suggest that we ought not to rule out regular and somewhat obligatory kinship interaction.

All the themes in our thinking about kinship that we have discussed so far—equalitarian versus kinship norms, the role of the opportunity structure, sporadic and voluntary kinship relations—presume that we know what is the minimal level of activity among relatives not sharing the same household that is necessary to provide an adequate basis for a social relationship. Rosow (1965:375) has clearly pointed out this problem by arguing that ritual visitations, ceremonial observances, and assistance in emergencies is not at all synonymous with stable, continual contact among kin. Although patterns of aid and support, claims of the relative importance of social relationships with kin, and organizations developing among kin are all predicated upon interaction, Rosow's observations are particularly acute in view of the measures of kin interaction and kin importance used in most research.

There are more studies of aid and support flowing among kin than there are of the frequency of their interaction. In studies that do examine interaction frequency among kin, there is a general reliance on "usual contact scores." In fact the findings of many studies of relationships that occur among kin have been brought into question by Mirande (1968:153-161), who used a more sensitive measure of interaction with kin—the number of hours weekly spent with relatives and the number of relatives seen.[a]

In view of these considerations, our own study employs as sensitive a measure of kin contact as possible. Thus, respondents were asked the frequency of contacts with each relative they reported as living outside of their household but within metropolitan Philadelphia in the seven days preceding the interview. It is assumed that this was a normal week in the lives of these people. While the restriction of information to a specific period of time may not convey an entirely representative picture of each individual's usual pattern of interaction with his kin, it avoids the problem of estimation on the part of the respondents. But most important, by directing our attention to the extent that relatives were seen within a limited time period, this procedure permits us to examine a set of actual choices exercised by these respondents in selecting which kin they did contact during a given week.

The focus of this chapter lies, then, with our respondents' interaction with geographically available kin, conceptualized in terms of recruitment of various kindred types. Our goal is to examine how the local opportunity structure of kinship is utilized by respondents, and how characteristics of this opportunity structure are associated with recruitment. In so doing, we shall see what the relative merits are of the thesis of an equalitarian emphasis and a kinship-based emphasis in the system of interaction among relatives. We shall assess the role that availability of kin plays in selection of relatives for interaction. And we shall try to gauge the independent effect on interaction of geographical distance between individuals and their relatives.

We shall ask such questions as the following: What differences, if any, are there in contact with specific types of kindred? What differences are there in the utilization of the opportunity structure of kinship on the basis of the specific kinship roles represented in a person's pool of relatives, or are relatives who occupy different kinship roles equally likely to be seen? How does the number of available kindred types and of representatives of different kindred types affect the number of kindred types contacted? Do people for whom representatives of various kindred types are unavailable compensate or substitute by turning to the relatives who are available, or are they less likely to see relatives at all? What is the relationship between interaction and the various residential distances separating respondents and their kin?

---

[a]Mirande's use of these more sensitive measures led to findings that support aspects of the thesis of the isolation of the family from kin. For example, social mobility was found to be disruptive of kin ties. Also, middle class people were found to have less contact with kin than working class people.

Availability and Interaction:
The Number of Kindred Types

The segment of an individual's universe of kin that comprises his pool of available relatives forms an opportunity structure for purposes of interaction. Considerable use of this opportunity structure was made by an overwhelming number of this working class sample. Over 80 percent of the 1,434 respondents with relatives living in metropolitan Philadelphia saw at least one relative in the seven-day period preceding the interview (this amounted to 1,172 respondents). And of the 15,695 relatives reported within the metropolitan area, about half, or 7,376, were seen during that week. This simple enumeration of kin seen by respondents indicates that the gross extent to which social relationships occur among relatives is considerable.

In this context, then, we can address the major question we have raised: What is the basis upon which relatives are recruited for interaction? And as a first approximation to an answer, we examine the role the opportunity structure of available kindred plays in recruitment. Are relatives recruited in such a way that people with a larger number of kindred types available to them are more likely to see relatives than people for whom the opportunity is more limited, for whom fewer kindred types are available? Do respondents with fewer choices compensate by seeing more representatives of those kindred types which are available, or does lack of choice mean that relatives are not seen? Data relevant to these questions are presented in Table 3-1.

In the second column of Table 3-1, the respondents who saw no relatives are arrayed by the number of kindred types available to them. This column shows that isolation from kin is negatively associated with the number of kindred types that comprise the respondent's pool of relatives. When people have only one or two kindred types available to them, they tend to be isolated in larger proportions than do those with more kindred types available to them. Thirty-four percent of those with one kindred type available are isolated, but only 18 percent of those with two kindred types available are isolated, while almost 10 percent of those with three and not quite 2 percent of those with four kindred types available are isolated. This amounts to a total of 262 isolated people—half the number of which (137) have one available kindred type only.

The converse of the negative association between isolation and number of kindred types available is a positive association—Gamma = + .55—between having any contact at all with kin and the number of available types. However, this association tells us nothing about the variety of kindred types seen under conditions of sparse or plentiful supply of these categories of relatives. Is, for instance, a variety of kindred types in the opportunity structure associated with greater selectivity in the recruitment of kin for interaction? Table 3-1 shows that while more respondents with a variety of kindred types saw some rather than none of their relatives, fewer respondents with many available kindred types saw representatives of them all. In fact, the smaller the number of kindred types the

Table 3-1
Respondents Who Saw Specific Numbers of Kindred Types by Number of Types Available (In Percentages)

Number of of Available Kindred Types	Proportion of of Available Types Seen	Number of Kindred Types Seen					
		None	One	Two	Three	Four	Total
One	.66	34.0 (137)	66.1 (267)				100.0 (404)
Two	.61	18.0 (83)	41.1 (189)	40.9 (188)			100.0 (460)
Three	.61	9.7 (39)	28.2 (113)	32.2 (129)	29.9 (120)		100.00 (401)
Four	.61	1.8 (3)	24.9 (42)	18.3 (31)	36.1 (61)	18.9 (32)	100.0 (169)
Total		(262)	(611)	(348)	(181)	(32)	(1434)

larger the proportion of respondents who saw representatives of all available kindred types. Thus, while two-thirds of those with one kindred type available saw kin of that type, about 41 percent of those with two kindred types available saw relatives of both types, about 30 percent of those with three types saw all three, and only about 19 percent of people with four kindred types available saw all four. All this indicates that although having a great variety of kinship roles available insures some interaction with relatives, it is less likely that these working class individuals will thereby have contact with each and every available kindred type.

However, it does not necessarily follow that respondents with more numerous kindred types available are being more selective in their recruitment of kin for interaction. To settle this question, we must look at the proportion of available kindreds seen. (Whether one or more than one representative of *each* kindred type was seen, of course, is not at issue here.)

The proportion of available kindred seen may be defined by:

$$P_j = \frac{x_i \, n_x}{N_j \, J}$$

where: x_i = the number of kindred types seen, i ranging from zero to J.

n_x = the number of respondents reporting x_i kindred types seen.

J = the number of kindred types in the pool of relatives.

N_j = the number of respondents reporting j kindred types available.

The proportion of kindred types seen by the number available is presented in the first column of Table 3-1. If respondents having a greater number of types of kindred available are more selective than respondents with fewer types available, then the proportion of kindred types seen would decrease as the number available increased. However, the proportion of kindred types seen remains constant at about two-thirds, on the average, regardless of the number of types available. Respondents with more types of kindred available do not see a smaller proportion of available types. Or, put another way, the constant *proportion* of kindred types seen indicates that respondents with more types available see a greater *number* of types of kindred than respondents with fewer types available. Greater variety of choice does not mean greater selectivity of types of relatives; it means that the possibility of recruiting a more varied set of kindred types is realized.

What then is the role of the opportunity structure of kindred types in the recruitment of kin for interaction? Variety of choice in the opportunity structure has a dual significance in the working class. Limitations on the variety of available kinship roles does not mean that respondents will see more, proportionately, of those types of kindred which are available. The consequence of limited kinship opportunity structure is not compensation, but isolation—that is, a greater likelihood that relatives will not be seen at all. While more respondents with greater choice were less likely to be isolated from all kin and more likely to see a greater variety of kindred types, at the same time fewer of them (proportionately) interact with the full number of types of kindred available to them. This is reflected in the inverse relation between the number of types of kindred and seeing all types available which is shown in the body of Table 3-1.

All told, the evidence shows that a large number of kin, and a variety of them, were seen by many respondents within the seven days preceding the interview. And it suggests that whether any relatives are seen and the number and variety of types seen is associated in a particular manner with the array of choices provided by the kinship roles in the respondent's pool of relatives. One way to view this formal aspect of kinship interaction is to think of it as a structural dimension along which at least the possibility of cultural constraints of kinship rather than equalitarian emphases are manifest. However, it must be emphasized that at the present this is surmise. The question of the extent to which this pattern of recruitment rests on equalitarian or kinship norms cannot be answered definitely by the data presented so far. That is, we do not know whether particular kindred types are favored for interaction. The richness of the opportunity structure of kindred types, although an indication of the number and variety of available kinship roles, is to this point simply an indication of the framework of interaction, not its content.

Availability and Interaction:
Specific Kindred Types

These data, therefore, will be supplemented by analysis of a second characteristic of the respondent's pool of relatives: the specific types of kindred represented therein. It will thus be possible to examine the role kindred type plays in whether such relatives are seen. If there is no pattern of kinship deference according to which an individual sees relatives, each type of kindred would be as likely to be seen as each other type, availability controlled.

The proportion of respondents who saw specific types of kindred when varying numbers of kindred types were available to them is shown in Table 3-2. The bottom row of Table 3-2 records the proportion of people who saw at least one relative of each kindred type regardless of how many kindred types were available to them. This row of the table indicates that there are major differences in the recruitment of relatives for interaction depending on their kindred type. Each type of kindred is not equally likely to be seen. Of the 781 respondents with joint descendant kindred available, 87 percent actually saw them. The proportion of respondents who saw joint descendants is far greater than the proportion who saw any other kindred type. On the other hand, distant kindred were seen by the smallest proportion of respondents, about 45 percent. The proportions of respondents who saw close kindred and spouse's kindred fall between these two extremes, 60 and 54 percent, respectively.

The three kindred types comprising an individual's bilateral kindred are close, distant, and joint descendant. The fact that more respondents saw close kindred (about 60 percent) than distant kindred (about 45 percent) is consistent with the view that genealogical considerations of distance among consanguineous relatives is important in determining whether they are recruited for interaction. However, the bottom row of Table 3-2 reveals an additional consideration suggesting a special feature of the fit between recruitment and genealogical distance. There is a differential pattern of recruitment of genealogically close but generationally distinct representatives of the bilateral kindred: a higher proportion of respondents saw joint descendants than saw close kindred.

Although the three kindred types comprising the respondent's bilateral kindred are not equally likely to be seen, almost as many respondents recruited spouse's kindred, about 54 percent, as close kindred, about 60 percent. A principle of symmetry about the affinal-consanguinal line appears to be operative in recruitment of close and spouse's kindred. That is, the thesis that there is a normative pattern of treating both an individual's close kindred (kin of orientation) and his spouse's close kindred (kin of orientation) equally is given some support on the basis of the percent of respondents who saw at least one representative of these two distinct kindred types.

Therefore, the differences we find in recruitment by type of kindred do not support the view that there is an equalitarian treatment for purposes of

Table 3-2
Respondents Who Saw Specific Kindred Types by the Number
of Kindred Types Available (In Percentages)

Number of Kindred Types Available	Kindred Type Seen			
	Close Kindred	Spouse's Kindred	Distant Kindred	Joint Descendant Kindred
One	53.4 (115)	52.5 (40)	31.4 (51)	84.8 (198)
Two	61.3 (310)	57.8 (142)	46.0 (280)	87.2 (188)
Three	63.2 (340)	57.9 (280)	44.8 (357)	85.8 (226)
Four	58.6 (169)	48.5 (169)	47.3 (169)	91.1 (169)
Respondents who saw specific available kindred types	60.4 (934)	54.4 (631)	44.9 (857)	87.1 (781)

interaction of *all* geographically available relatives—regardless of the kinship role they represent. The findings of other studies regarding the role that genealogical distance and generational differences play in recruitment of representatives of one's own bilateral kindred are strongly supported by these findings. Equal or symmetrical treatment of one's own kindred and one's spouse's kindred for interaction, however, is also a feature of a recruitment system based on kinship relation.

We now must also examine whether there are differences in contact with specific types of kindred when other types of kindred are and are not available. This issue is important because the associations reported in Table 3-1 between the number of types of kindred available and the number seen may disguise large differences in recruitment pattern by kindred type. That is, patterns of recruitment of specific kindred may be quite different among respondents for whom numerous types of kindred are absent in comparison to those for whom a variety of types from which to choose are present. Put differently, equalitarianism in the recruitment of kin for interaction may only be operative when respondents are limited in their choices, while selectivity based on kinship considerations may apply to those who have a variety of kindreds in the opportunity structure.

The number of respondents who saw specific types of kindred by the number of types of kindred that comprise their pool of available relatives can be examined in Table 3-2. The table reveals that regardless of the number of kindred types comprising the pool of relatives of these respondents, the pattern of recruitment of specific kindred remains consistent. Despite the number of other kindred types in these respondents' pools of relatives, the highest proportion saw joint descendants and the lowest proportion saw distant kindred—that is, saw at least one such relative. The proportion who saw close kindred and spouse's kindred falls between these two extremes. There are some minor differences among respondents who saw specific kindred depending on the number of other types comprising their pool of relatives. For example, there is a slight tendency for smaller proportions of respondents with one than with two or more available kindred types to see any relatives at all. This is most evident when distant kindred are the only available relatives. Also, when all four kindred types are available, spouse's kindred and distant kindred tend to be seen by about equally few respondents. Under these conditions of maximum freedom of choice in recruitment of kin, equalitarian norms may or may not be present in some form, but if present they nevertheless do not alter the main interaction pattern, which is kindred based.

On the whole, the data arrayed in Table 3-2 lends additional support to the view that a major basis underlying the selection of available relatives is the type of kindred involved in the interaction with the respondents. Equalitarian treatment is not the *general* rule in recruitment. Moreover, the data reinforce the finding reported in the previous section that these working class respondents neither compensate for the absence of a variety of choice nor are they pulled from associations with specific kindred when other types are available. The integrity—in this sense—of the social relationships with each type of kindred remains constant. Available relatives are not equally likely to be seen when their kinship relation to the respondent is taken into account. It therefore seems evident that selection of kin for interaction does not depend, in the main, on socioemotional compatibility.

Geographical Distance and Interaction

The question of the equalitarian versus the kinship basis of the system of social relations among kin does not rest solely on whether there is an association between the kinship roles that relatives occupy and the social interaction between them and our respondents. Other factors, which in themselves may have little to do with kinship and which are extraneous to the recruitment of kin qua kin, may nevertheless influence interaction among relatives. We will consider one of these factors, geographical distance from the respondent of the residences of his relatives. Relatives who live at some distance within the metropolitan area may not be seen, or may be seen less frequently, compared to relatives who live close by. If the dispersion of kin does indeed serve to lessen kinship interaction in this way, then of course, a crucial question must be asked of the social relations of our respondents and their kin. How much, if any, does geographical distance from kin disrupt the pattern of relationships we have found between the type of kindred a relative represents and interaction with that relative?

Table 3-3 provides part of the answer. The proportion of working class people who see relatives representative of various kindred types is markedly affected by whether they live within six blocks of, or six blocks or more from, their residences. More people see their relatives if they are nearby. There is about a 25 percent difference between the proportion of our respondents who see close and spouse's kindred, depending on how far away they live. The difference is about 29 percent where distant kindred are concerned. And it falls to about 14 percent for joint descendants. Furthermore, if one compares the information about the proportion of respondents seeing various kindred types depending on the number of such types available in the metropolitan area (which can be found in Table 3-2), a certain similarity of effect can be observed between greater distance and lesser availability of kindred types. Almost identical proportions of these working class people see each of their kindred types if, on the one hand, these relatives live six or more blocks away, or if, on the other hand, there is only one kindred type available. One might say that the impact of a limited opportunity structure upon kinship interaction is about the same as that of greater geographical distance. Both these conditions put the proportion of people interacting with their various types of kindred within one to five percentage points of each other.

However, what is equally important, Table 3-3 reveals that the impact of geographical distance, although considerable in terms of the greater or lesser proportion of people seeing a particular kindred type, is negligible in terms of the *pattern* of interaction. That is, while the overall proportions of these working class people who contact each of their various types of kindred may be high if they live nearby and low if they live at some distance, the proportion of people who interact with one kindred type as compared to another kindred type still depends on what type of kindred is in question and not on geographical distance. For, as Table 3-3 clearly shows, whether relatives live close at hand or far away, the proportion of respondents who saw joint descendant kindred is still far greater than the proportion who saw any other type, and distant kindred

Table 3-3
Respondents Who Saw Various Kindred by
Geographical Distance (In Percentages)

Geographical Distance	Close Kindred	Spouse's Kindred	Distant Kindred	Joint Descendants
Within six blocks	77.2 (259)	72.5 (160)	65.2 (247)	96.0 (251)
Six blocks or more	52.3 (833)	47.8 (566)	36.5 (758)	82.3 (666)

were still seen by the smallest proportion of respondents. Close and spouse's kindred fall between these two extremes—with slightly larger proportions of people seeing close than spouse's kindred.

This is precisely the order of kinship deference observed (see the bottom line of Table 3-2) among our respondents without regard to geographical distance or numerosity of available kindred types; and it is precisely the pattern of kinship interaction maintained by these working class people regardless of the number of kindred types available (see the body of Table 3-2). These results, then, specify the limited respect in which it is true that in our society, factors extraneous to kinship itself have a bearing on the system of kinship interaction. Both the number of kindred types available and geographical distance from kindred influence the degree to which people participate in social interaction with their relatives, but do not affect the patterns of recruitment of kin for interaction. Thus far, patterns of recruitment would seem to be a matter involving norms of kinship: some types of kindred are seen by larger proportions of working class people than others under any conditions of availability or distance.

Insofar as it involves geographical distance, this matter can be clarified further. Up to this point we have not shown how the element of choice or the lack of it relates to the dampening effect of geographical distance on kinship interaction. That is, we have not examined the interrelations between geographical distance, kinship interaction, and kindred type. Is there a process of selectivity based on geographical distance in the recruitment of kin? Or do larger proportions of people see their kin when they live nearby because they have no relatives of the same kindred type who live farther away? To resolve this issue we need to know not only the geographical distance of representatives of each kindred type from our respondents, but also whether a respondent has such a relative in one geographical area or both.

In Table 3-4, geographical distance is divided into two areas—within six blocks, and six blocks or more. The table arrays data on contact with specific kindred types by geographical distance for those working class people who have such relatives available in both areas and for those who only have kin in one of the two areas. By considering each kindred type separately in Table 3-4, it is clear that interaction with each specific category of relative is not influenced by the fact that such a relative is represented in both geographical areas: the proportion of respondents who will contact that relative is unaffected. Almost identical proportions of our respondents see their kin who live nearby whether or not another relative of that type lives farther away. Within each kindred type, the principle by which kin are selected does not depend on the choices available; it depends on sheer distance. For example, consider those working class people with close kindred who live nearby (within six blocks). Seventy-eight percent of them who also had close kindred living farther away contacted the relative close by. But about the same proportion, 76 percent, whose only close kindred lived nearby contacted such a nearby relative. Consider now those respondents whose

Table 3-4
Respondents Who Saw Kindred Types by Geographical Distance,
Among Those with Kindred in Both and Only One Area
(In Percentages)

Geographical Distance	Availability of Kindred	Close Kindred	Spouse's Kindred	Distant Kindred	Joint Descendant Kindred
Within six blocks	Has kindred in both areas	78.0 (159)	74.1 (85)	62.4 (149)	95.6 (136)
	Only kindred in this area	76.0 (100)	70.7 (75)	69.4 (98)	96.5 (115)
Six blocks or more	Has kindred in both areas	54.1 (159)	49.4 (85)	44.3 (149)	82.4 (136)
	Only kindred in this area	51.9 (674)	47.6 (471)	34.6 (609)	82.4 (530)

only close kindred lived six blocks or more from them. About 52 percent of these people saw such a relative. And if a respondent with close kindred that far away also had close kindred nearby, still an almost identical proportion, 54 percent, saw close kindred who lived far away.

The analogous finding is displayed in Table 3-4 for each kindred type. Whether spouse's, distant, or joint descendant kindred are being contacted, almost identical proportions of people see the nearby relatives whether or not they have a choice between nearby or geographically more distant kin; and, almost identical proportions of people see kin living relatively far away whether or not they have this choice. The great difference resides in the fact that, choice or no, smaller proportions of people contact geographically distant kin. As we would expect, there is no change in the pattern of interaction which we have found in the preceding analysis to be characteristics of these working class people. Whether nearby or geographically distant relatives are seen, whether there is a choice of relatives in another geographical area or not, still the largest proportion of respondents interact with their joint descendent kindred, the smallest proportion interact with their distant kindred, and in between these extremes about the same proportion of people interact with their close and spouse's kindred.

As Tables 3-3 and 3-4 show, the effects of geographical distance on contact with kin require careful interpretation. While geographical distance between an individual and his relatives places constraints on contact, the selection of which type of kindred to see is not dependent on where they live. Having a relative representing a specific kindred type living nearby does not mean that those with the same kinship role living farther away are not seen. The absence of relatives nearby does not mean that geographically distant kin are more likely to be seen. Rather, there would appear to be a gradient of contact, depending on where relatives live, but a gradient that lessens the overall level of interaction without disturbing the order of kinship deference. These working class people neither compensate for the absence of kindred nearby by seeing those who live farther away, nor do they neglect to see kin who are not in their locale because they have other relatives living nearby.

The Extent and Frequency of Interaction
and Geographical Distance

One further question must be answered in order to clarify the preceding analysis. How much contact occurs among these relatives? So far we have shown how characteristics of the local opportunity structure of available relatives are related to whether any kin are seen at all. Having already demonstrated how both geographical distance and the type of kindred a relative represents bear on contact (in this sense of no interaction versus any interaction), now it is necessary to evaluate the role that relatives play in working class people's daily lives as indicated by their extent and frequency of interaction with their kin. Do respondents simply keep in minimal touch with one representative of available kindred or are there more frequent contacts with a larger number of these relatives? How is geographical distance from kin related to the number of relatives seen and frequency of contact?

The analysis in previous sections indicated that certain types of relatives are seen by greater proportions of people than others, and that the overall level of such contact is influenced by where they live. Now, in looking beyond the dichotomy of contact or no contact, we will be able to see if respondents also interact with a large number of representatives of some kindred types as opposed to others; and we can evaluate more closely the effects of geographical distance on kinship relations. Does geographical distance influence the number of relatives seen and the frequency of interaction of specific kindred types, or is its significance limited to the dampening effect on the proportion of people who have any contact at all with kin, which we have already observed?

Our analysis of these questions must be prefaced by some procedural remarks. The answers we seek require us to supplement the kind of information thus far presented by making use of elaborate data dealing with interaction in terms of the number of relatives of each kindred type seen and the frequency of contact with them. For any particular respondent the number of kin seen and frequency of contact, by kindred type, is limited by whether the area is richly or sparsely supplied with each such category of relative. So that the different sizes of various individual's kindred types will not preclude analysis, the data on frequency of contact with kin and number of kin seen will each be presented in the form of an index that will statistically account for the number of available representatives of a particular kindred type.[b] The rationale for these measures stems from the difficulty of comparing individuals with the same type but different sized kindred. If each respondent had reported only one representative of a kindred type available to him, then the mean number of relatives seen and the frequency of interaction for each type of kindred could be examined for the sample as a whole with little difficulty.

But since most respondents reported more than one representative of these kindred types available to them, we will reduce this number of available relatives to the base of one. That is, the mean number of kin seen and the mean frequency of interaction with kin can be represented for the sample as a whole by the use of an index that has the property of accounting for the number of representatives of a kindred statistically by reducing this number to the base of one. This index can be defined thus:

$$\frac{\sum \dfrac{\bar{x}_i n_i}{X_i}}{N}$$

where:

$\bar{x}_i$ = the mean number seen (or mean frequency of interaction) of the number available.

n_i = the number of respondents who reported X_i kindred.

X_i = the number of representatives of a kindred type available to a respondent.

N = the total number of respondents reporting one or more representatives of a specific kindred type available

In essence, the index provides a weighted mean, transformed to a base of one, of either the number of relatives seen or the frequency of interaction per available relative—and hence a measure of either of these two separate dimensions of recruitment *for the sample as a whole*.

Both these dimensions of kinship interaction are shown in Table 3-5. (The upper limit of the index measuring mean frequency of contact is seven, since

[b]The presence in the sample of different-sized kindreds can be approached in two ways. By sorting on size, the number of representatives of a particular kindred type can be controlled, and comparisons between kindreds among respondents with like-sized kindreds can be made. This approach yields confirmation of our previous findings. In terms of the number of kin seen and the frequency of interaction, joint descendants are contacted most, distant kindred least, and close and spouse's kindred with similar levels of contact fall between these extremes. However, sorting on size does not permit us to make comparisons for the sample as a whole—only for those with like-sized kindreds. Hence we employ a second approach, which will account statistically for different-sized kindreds and represent the number of kin seen and the frequency of interaction by indices for the entire sample. (See Anspach, 1970.)

Table 3-5
Extent and Frequency of Contact with Specific Kindred Types by Geographical Distance

Geographical Distance	Close Kindred			Spouse's Kindred			Distant Kindred			Joint Descendant Kindred		
	Mean Number Seen[a]	Mean Frequency of Contact[b]	(N)	Mean Number Seen	Mean Frequency of Contact	(N)	Mean Number Seen	Mean Frequency of Contact	(N)	Mean Number Seen	Mean Frequency of Contact	(N)
Within six blocks	.71	2.19	(259)	.65	2.01	(160)	.60	1.74	(247)	.89	3.54	(251)
Six blocks or more	.39	.57	(833)	.33	.48	(556)	.21	.30	(758)	.67	1.32	(666)
Total	.43	.91	(934)[c]	.39	.62	(631)	.27	.52	(857)	.72	.52	(781)

[a]Range = 0-1
[b]Range = 0-7
[c]The (N) appearing in the Total row represents all respondents with this kindred in the metropolitan area. Since some respondents have representatives of a kindred in both areas, this figure will not equal the sum of (N)s within the table.

interaction is being measured for the seven-day period prior to interview). The bottom row of the table presents totals for the entire sample without accounting for the geographical distance of kin. These results are consistent with the findings reported in Table 3-2 (which was concerned with whether any contact at all occurred). That is, the present data show that the available opportunity structure of close, distant, spouse's, and joint descendant kindred are utilized differentially in terms of the mean frequency of interaction and the mean number seen. More joint descendants were seen and they were contacted more frequently than any other kindred type. Fewer of the distant kindred of these working class people were seen than any other kindred type, and they were contacted less frequently than any other kindred type. And close and spouse's kindred fall between these two extremes.

Our previous findings did not refute the view that one's own close kindred and one's spouse's kindred are treated equally in terms of whether any of these relatives are seen at all. But it requires more careful examination to determine whether it is also true that the opportunity structure of available close and spouse's kindred are equally utilized in terms of number and frequency. The bottom row in Table 3-5 indicates that it depends on which dimension of interaction is being discussed. While there is little difference between the mean *number* of close and spouse's kindred seen, the mean *frequency* of contact with close kindred is greater than with spouse's kindred: close kindred were seen about one and one-half times more frequently than spouse's kindred. This suggests that while respondents follow the kinship norm of making no invidious distinction between these types of kindred by seeing as many relatives of both types, they nevertheless have more contacts with their own close kindred. Equal or symmetrical treatment? In part, yes. However, despite kinship norms which enjoin symmetry, people in the working class favor their own close kindred by seeing them more intensively.

How then does geographical distance influence the number of kin seen and the frequency with which they are seen? Table 3-5 clearly reinforces the findings presented so far. The greater geographical distance of working class people from their kin does serve to dampen or reduce the proportion of respondents who see them. In addition, the number of our respondents' kin who are seen and the frequency with which they are seen is also dampened or reduced. Moreover, the dampening effect of geographical distance is stronger on the frequency of interaction than on the number of relatives seen. For example, the ratio between the mean number of close kindred seen who live nearby, to those far away from respondents is less than 2:1; while almost four times as many contacts occurred with close kindred living within six blocks for every contact with close kindred living six or more blocks away. (Analogous differences can be found for each of the other kindred types by consulting the body of Table 3-5.)

But as before, the effect of geographical distance is not strong enough to alter the order that kinship norms impose on interaction with relatives representing specific kindred types. No matter where they live, nearby or at a distance, joint descendant kindred are contacted by the greatest proportion of respondents. Also, as we now see, joint descendant kindred are the category from which the largest mean number of relatives are contacted. Furthermore it is the kindred type in which is found the greatest mean frequency of contact per relative. Whether they live nearby or farther away, fewer representatives of distant kindred are seen and the frequency of interaction per representative of distant kindred is less than for any other kindred type. Close and spouse's kindred remain between these two extremes no matter how far away they live from our working class respondents.

Conclusion

It seems clear from the analysis of kinship interaction in this chapter that neither the principle of equalitarianism nor that of consanguinity and genealogical distance suffice to describe recruitment in the relational system of kinship. The evidence suggests that the way the relational system of kinship operates has not been properly understood. There is a clear ordering of recruitment of kin for interaction according to the kinship role occupied by a person's relative in the working class. Yet at the same time, and without altering this order, the level of utilization of kin is affected by factors extraneous to kinship itself, factors which in principle permit the play of equalitarian criteria in kinship interaction. Both sets of criteria are involved in social relations with kin, but they are involved in different ways. Factors extraneous to kinship, such as geographical distance, place constraints on all kin contact; the selection of one particular relative as against another for interaction, however, is not based on such considerations. Recruitment remains kindred-based, depending on the type of genealogical linkage characterizing an individual and his relatives.

A hint of the essentially kindred-based pattern of interaction with relatives reveals itself first in the less than maximal usage of the opportunity structure of available kindred types. Under conditions of limited opportunity, where only one or two kindred types are available, the proportion of those isolated from all relatives is larger by a substantial amount than under conditions of greatest opportunity where many or all kindred types are available. Apparently, rather than compensate for the absence of certain categories of kin by seeing those who are available, some do not interact at all with relatives. Under conditions of greatest opportunity, where the largest number of kindred types are available, smaller proportions of respondents interact with representatives of *all* available types. Thus, working class people exhibit both a preference for isolation when opportunities are restricted to few kindred types, and a disinclination to see all available types of kin when the opportunities are more varied.

Both these patterns of utilization of the opportunity structure imply the existence of norms preventing compensatory kin behavior as well as indiscriminate interaction in the relational system of kinship. Yet between these extremes of the minimum and maximum utilization of the opportunity structure of kindred types there is a sense in which a presumably kindred-based selectivity is affected by the richness of the opportunity structure. For the more kindred types available, the more likely is it that a variety of types of kindred will be seen by these working class people: this is indexed by the constant *proportion* of kindred types seen no matter how many are available—and hence the larger *number* seen when more are available.

One may say of this increasing variety in kin interaction that accompanies increasing availability of kindred types that it too reflects a feature of the kinship norms governing recruitment: kinship priorities order interaction with categories of kin in terms of relative importance. When other kindred types are available, those of least kinship importance may not be seen, or few may see them. If kindred types of greatest importance are not available, but those least important are, no kin may be seen in preference to contacting those of least importance. But when there is a relatively wide range of opportunities among the available kindred types, then a more varied set of kin may be recruited for interaction, with the emphasis on the more important categories of relatives.

The kindred-based linkage system of interaction places joint descendant kindred first in order of priority. More representatives of joint descendants are recruited by a larger proportion of respondents for whom such kinship roles are available, and they are seen more frequently than any other type of kindred. Since the kinship roles comprising joint descendant kindred consist of the respondent's adult children, their in-marrying affines, and their collective children, these findings provide a structural basis—in the working class—for Sussman's view that other than relations with those kin residing in the same household, relationships between parents and their adult children are the most affective kinship bonds in our society. Among the other kindred types comprising an individual's bilateral kindred, close and distant kindred are, respectively, second and third in order of magnitude on all dimensions of recruitment for interaction.

The order of recruitment among bilateral kindred types confirms the theoretically derived decision to separate genealogically close relatives into two distinct kindred types based on generation: joint descendant and close. The consistently higher proportions of respondents seeing joint descendants than close kindred reveals a behavioral differentiation in kinship which is often ignored theoretically. Doubtless this failure to distinguish in theory between those categories of kin we have termed close and joint descendant stems from kinship nomenclature considerations, wherein these relatives are terminologically similarly related, even though occupying generationally distinct kinship roles.

At this point, of course, one has the option of interpreting this pattern of interaction in terms of the looseness of fit between cultural and social systems of kinship. However, we believe this to be an error that throws the blame for loose conceptualization upon the social structure. We prefer to think that the fact that categories of relatives comprising a respondent's own bilateral kindred are not equally likely to be seen is an example of priorities inherent in the culture of kinship, as well as manifest in interaction. In this respect it seems quite convincing that the opportunity structure of distant kindred is least utilized for interaction by the sample as a whole.

From the emphasis on bilaterality and the division of kindreds into kindred types, it follows that the category of kin we have termed spouse's kindred would be recruited in a manner similar to the corresponding set of consanguineous kin of ego. Under our typology of kindreds, this is respondent's close kin. Hence we also view the symmetry of recruitment between these two kindred types as a feature of the culture of kinship as well as the relational system of kinship. There is no reason to assume that these similar rates of interaction between spouse's and close kindred reflect a looseness in the fit between culture and social system.

However, not all of the variability we have observed can be interpreted as a function of kinship per se. The very marked lowering of the level of interaction with kin who live within the metropolitan area, but not close by, is indicative of the effects of equalitarian norms—but in a particular way. Since the order of kinship preference is not changed by geographical distance, but the overall level at which the relational system of kinship operates is simply reduced, geographical distance appears to be a factor extraneous to kinship yet applying fairly uniformly to social relations with all categories of kin. The claim for the functioning of equalitarian norms in kinship relations is justified in this sense.

On the basis of these findings we are driven to conclude that the question of whether equalitarian or kinship norms govern kinship interaction is no longer a meaningful one. Obviously they are both major factors in the recruitment of kin. In terms of some old but hardly obsolete concepts: *gemeinschaft* and *gesellschaft* elements coexist as major factors in one and the same contemporary, urban social system. Perhaps we have grown accustomed to thinking of them as mutually opposed or contradictory features in the context of modern societies. If so, this is an error. The obligations of kinship appear to survive in a relational system whose overall level of functioning is substantially influenced by that most *gesellschaftlich* and "equalitarian" of criteria—convenience, as measured by geographic distance.

Aside from lack of theoretical insight, how could those who espouse the equalitarian position have come to their view? We suspect their methodology may be involved. Some of these researchers rely on individual subjects as informants. Each such subject reports seeing particular combinations of representatives of kinship roles, and is compared with other subjects for traces of common interaction sets. Variation in size of kindreds, and failure to take account of differential availability of kinship roles, lend a spurious sense of randomness to the patterns of behavior observed. This approach is by its nature one that tends to emphasize the idiosyncratic aspects of individual cases. The inherent bias of the informant methodology is made more severe by the failure to employ aggregate data. Common patterns of interaction based on kinship relations cannot be found without systematic aggregation of categories of kin as well as categories of egos.

Finally, we return to the one remaining general issue concerning the nature of kinship, which was introduced at the beginning of this chapter. Are the relationships that occur among kin sporadic and voluntary or regular and obligatory? In part, the question has already been answered. But also in part, our data are hardly sufficient to provide a fully satisfactory answer. An obvious limitation is the brief period of time about which we questioned respondents concerning kin contact. Nevertheless, some further light can be shed on the issue, always keeping in mind that the question of whether rates of interaction are sufficient evidence of regular or sporadic relationships with kin depends on the criteria utilized. Our data indicate that the question whether relationships with available kin are sporadic or regular is a poor one. The answer to the question as stated is that they are both sporadic and regular or intense. It depends on the type(s) of kindred(s) available. If distant kindred are the only available relatives, interaction patterns are likely to be sporadic. Relationships with joint descendant kindred, on the other hand, are most likely to be regular and intense.

4

Kinship Interaction and the Life Cycle

In the analysis of kinship interaction of the preceding chapter, we concentrated our attention on characteristics of the relatives of these working class people such as their availability and their kinship relation to the respondents. In this chapter the emphasis changes from characteristics of relatives to characteristics of respondents. We will focus on the stage of the life cycle at which a person has arrived. And the age and the marital status of the respondents will serve as life cycle indicators for our purposes. In this chapter, then, our goal is to determine how age and marital status are related to the problem of explaining variability in kinship behavior. Data will be presented on the interrelationships between these characteristics of the people in our sample and their contacts with various kindred types. As will be seen, this material not only suggests how social relationships with kin may change as they are worked out during the life cycle, but also has major implications concerning how working class kinship systems operate.

Integration and Flexibility of the Relational System of Kinship

The data to be presented in this chapter will permit us to examine two related issues dealing with working class kinship. The first issue concerns the identification of key kinship roles which are central to the operation of the relational system, while the second issue concerns the flexibility of the system itself.

First we will determine whether the aged are central figures in the relational system of kinship. A number of sociologists have drawn attention to the role that older people play in relationships that occur among kin. Adams (1968:169), in summarizing his own findings as well as those of others, claims that the aged are the foci of urban kin relations. However, this claim is vague and lacks a sufficient empirical base. There are several ways the aged could be central figures in urban kin affairs: (1) relatives could interact with one another because of an older relative; (2) the relatives an individual sees could be older; or (3) older people could see more relatives more frequently, or see more of a variety of types of relatives than younger people, and thus serve to integrate the local kin network. This latter alternative is at issue here—the question pertaining to the integrative role that older people play in kin affairs.

The thesis that the aged are the foci of urban kinship in this sense lacks a sufficient empirical base. The claim is based on findings which indicate that adult children (who frequently serve as the sample of respondents, e.g., in Adams) and their parents maintain contacts with one another and are engaged in various forms of reciprocal exchange. Not only is the claim that the aged are central figures in the kinship system limited by the absence of a sample of older respondents themselves, but there is also a paucity of data concerning the relationships of older people with kin other than their adult children. Thus, whether parents serve an integrative function in kin affairs by serving as links between their children and other relatives cannot be known from previous studies. Moreover, the argument advanced in the preceding chapter leads us to believe in advance of any data on the relation between age and kin interaction that this matter concerns more than chronological age alone. That joint descendants are seen by most people would seem in good part to be due to kinship norms rather than age itself. The parental-filial set of roles and the obligations attaching to them would seem to be *a priori* as responsible for the relative interaction rates of middle-aged and older people with their offspring as either the fact of advanced years, or the free time it permits for family social relations, or the shift of attention from occupational to familial concerns brought about by the end or the approaching end of involvement with full-time employment, and the like.

The second issue concerns the flexibility of the relational system of kinship. We have shown (in Chapter 3) that, for the sample as a whole, there is regularity in patterns of contact depending on the type of kindred with whom interaction occurs. That a patterned relational structure exists, however, is only the first of several things we need to know about the relational system of kinship. The next aspect of the problem to be investigated is not structure or lack of it, but the flexibility of the relational system itself. We are concerned with whether the patterned differences we have observed in contact by type of kindred remain constant at the various stages of an individual's life cycle. Or does the pattern of kinship interaction fail to persist—that is, become less flexible—in the face of different or changing life circumstances of working class people? More specifically, is there differential utilization of the opportunity structures of available kindreds by respondents at different age levels and among those married and not married?

The possibility that shifts in recruitment from one type of kindred to another may occur among respondents at different ages is derived from two somewhat divergent points of view. First are the suggestions of Cumming and Schneider (1961:498-499) that due to the equalitarian emphasis among kindred, which permits selection of kin for interaction on nonkinship bases, and to the age-grading in our society that results in social distance between generations, there is a particular emphasis in our kinship system on social relations among collaterals—in particular siblings. Furthermore, they suggest (1961:504-505) that a shift in solidarity occurs through time, with older people often feeling closer to collaterals than to their adult children. While Cumming and Schneider do not report on interaction patterns, they do suggest that sibling solidarity may be a fundamental axis of socioemotional interaction among older people, especially in the last forty to fifty years of life. But Adams's (1968:165) findings on relationships among siblings are ambiguous with respect to Cumming and Schneider's viewpoint. Adams found that his sample of younger to middle aged respondents (ages 20 to 45) showed no tendency toward sibling solidarity. According to him, relationships between young adult siblings were to a large extent constrained by different values and interests. One might regard Adams's results as disconfirmation of the sibling solidarity thesis, or at best as only partial confirmation of the Cumming and Schneider version of it, in view of the lack of sibling solidarity in the first half to two-thirds of life.

The findings of Young and Wilmott also point to a shift in contacts with kin over time. However, their viewpoint is clearly opposed to Cumming and Schneider's. In their study of working class kinship relations in Great Britain, Young and Wilmott (1957:76-79) found that social relationships among siblings were attenuated after the deaths of parents. It would appear that upon the death of central kinship figures the relational system breaks down along the collateral dimension, and perhaps along others as well. Thus, while Cumming and Schneider would lead one to expect that older people are more likely to interact with their siblings than younger people, Young and Wilmott seem to suggest that older people are less likely to do so, since the death of parents removes the mediating linkage.

Our findings permit a somewhat direct examination of patterns of interaction among siblings. Siblings and siblings' spouses, along with living parents (of whom there are few in this sample), comprise respondents' close kindred. Cumming and Schneider's suggestions would lead us to expect that older respondents utilize the opportunity structure of available close kindred more extensively than do younger respondents. Their suggestions would also lead us to examine differential patterns of recruitment of joint descendants among different aged respondents and find that older people are less likely than younger people to see their adult children. Young and Wilmott's view, on the other hand, would suggest that the opportunity structure of close kindred, which contains siblings, is less extensively utilized among older people since their parents are not likely to be living.

The suggestions of Cumming and Schneider and those of Young and Wilmott are limited to considerations of shifts in recruitment of kin who comprise one's own bilateral kindred. We ask the additional question: is there differential utilization of the opportunity structure of spouse's kindred among respondents at different age levels? In particular, is there a turning away from spouse's kindred to representatives of one's own kindred with aging and the accompanying disruptions that occur in marriage? And, is there a differential utilization of the opportunity structures of close and spouse's kindred between respondents who were and were not married at the time of the interview.

The question of the association between marital status and contact with kin is particularly important in understanding how the relational system of kinship operates. Knowledge about this relationship will permit us to determine how cultural definitions of consanguinity and affinity are related to kinship interaction, if they are at all. According to Schneider (1968:80), deaths, divorces, and remarriages raise special problems with relationships with relatives who are considered as "inlaws," such as spouse's kindred. From his cultural account of American kinship, Schneider (1968:92) suggests that relationships with inlaws lack the binding permanence that relationships with one's own kindred entail. That is, there is some question as to whether upon the disruption of marriage, an individual will continue to recognize inlaws as kin or continue to maintain contacts with his former spouse's kindred. From the considerations presented in Chapter 1 regarding the kindred, the question must also be raised whether the disruption of marriage entails a reestablishment or continuation of social relationships with relatives who comprise one's own close kindred.

Age, Marital Status, and Availability of Kindred Types

Before turning to the findings on interaction, some background information will be presented concerning the relation between age and marital status and the composition of the respondent's pool of available relatives. Certain kinship roles are not as likely to be available to older respondents and to those not married as they are to those who are married and younger.

In Chapter 2 we examined the composition of the pool of relatives of the respondents in terms of the types of kindred represented and for our respondents as a whole. Since no one kindred type or combination of types was overwhelmingly modal for the sample, and since some types were absent for many, the local kinship structure was characterized as fragmented. We noted that factors associated with the geographical dispersion and propinquity occurring among relatives are complex—reflecting not only characteristics of the respondent in terms of his status-set, but of those of each of his relatives as well. While we presented no data, we did intimate that the age and marital status of the respondents were among the important determinants of which kinship roles will be occupied by living people in one's universe of kin and which relatives will live outside an individual's household. In this sample, we have already seen the age of respondents reflected in the small number of parents reported as living. The losses of occupants of kinship roles (due to deaths of aunts, uncles, parents and siblings) which is associated with an individual's advancing age are made up in role gains reflected in the births and marriages of an individual's descendants and his collaterals' descendants.

The question therefore arises whether the role losses and role gains associated with the age of the respondents are reflected in the composition of the pool of available kin and whether they thereby account for some of the variability previously noted in the types of kindred available. In order to answer this question, the sample was divided by age into those between 45 and 54 years, those between 55 and 64 years, and those 65 years and over. These are, respectively, 30, 30, and 40 percent of the respondents with kin in the metropolitan area. The association between age and whether each of the four types of kindreds are represented among the pool of available relatives is presented in Table 4-1.

Age is inversely related (Gamma:−.403) to having representatives of close kindred in the pool of available relatives. Age is also negatively associated (Gamma: −.340) with having representatives of one's spouse's kindred among the pool of available relatives. These inverse relationships are understandable as close kindred and spouse's kindred include only representatives of the respondent's generationally ascendent and collateral kin. As age of respondent reflects the losses through deaths of occupants of these kinship roles, the representation of such relatives in the pool of kin is thus affected.

For some respondents, the losses in the representation of close and spouse's kin in the pool of available relatives are made up in part by gains in joint descendants. For age is positively associated (Gamma: +.488) with joint descendants being represented in the pool of available relatives. This positive association occurs as a result of the respondent's children leaving the household, marrying and having children, but not leaving the metropolitan area.

So far, the interpretation of the measures of association reported are fairly obvious. However, the revelation in Table 4-1 that there is an inverse association between age (Gamma: −.320) and whether representatives of distant kindred are available is not easily explained by generational considerations. We previously

Table 4-1
Respondents Who Report Various Kindred Types Among
Their Pool of Available Relatives, by Age
(In Percentages)

Age	Close Kindred	Spouse's Kindred	Distant Kindred	Joint Descendant Kindred
65 and over	52.4 (580)	35.3 (580)	49.8 (580)	71.3 (580)
55-64	68.1 (423)	47.0 (423)	60.0 (423)	63.2 (423)
54 and under	79.4 (431)	60.8 (431)	72.8 (431)	32.8 (431)
Gamma	−.403	−.340	−.320	+.488

noted (Chapter 2) that while the role composition of distant kindred theoretically includes aunts, uncles, and grandparents, the overwhelming majority of kin
who comprise this type of kindred and who live in the metropolitan area are in
fact the respondent's nieces and nephews. Since most of the relatives comprising
distant kindred are the respondents' siblings' descendants, one would expect that
if age were at all associated with availability of these relatives it would be
positively. While we do not have all the evidence to support our view, what we
do possess suggests that the inverse relationship between age and the availability
of distant kindred occurs as a result of (1) geographical moves on the part of
some siblings' children upon leaving the parental household; (2) the deaths of
aunts, uncles and grandparents; and (3) the loss of contact by some respondents
with their distant kindred following the deaths of those close kindred who
served as connecting links between the two.

The pattern of availability of relatives for respondents of different ages can be
further elaborated. Those working class people who reported representatives of
various kindred types among their pool of available relatives can be examined in
terms of how many members of each kindred type were available to them and
whether this number is associated with their own age. We did this by first
determining the median number of relatives to be found in each type of kindred
reported in the metropolitan area, and then measuring the association between
respondents' age and having more than the median number of relatives of each
kindred type available. These associations between age and size of kindred type
are consistent with the associations just reported between age and whether any
representatives at all of the four types of kindred were available in the pool of
relatives in the metropolitan area. That is, among people having available
representatives of these kindred types, age is negatively associated with the
number of respondents who reported above the median of close kindred
(Gamma: $-.354$), spouse's kindred (Gamma: $-.479$), and distant kindred (Gamma: $-.294$). And age is positively associated with the number who reported
above the median of joint descendants (Gamma: $+.264$). Hence, not only do
fewer older people have representatives of any given kindred type when
compared to younger people, but also those relatives older people do have
available to them in any given kindred type are likely to be fewer in number
than the corresponding relatives of younger people.

It is also consistent with these findings that age is negatively associated
(Gamma: $-.207$) with the number of *types* of kindred that comprise the pool of
relatives available to these working class people. Thus with increasing age, there
is an atrophy of types of kindred available. For example, the largest proportion
of respondents who reported only one type of kindred in their pool of relatives
were 65 and over. These respondents represent over a third of the oldest age
cohort in the sample as compared with about 20 percent of respondents age 54
and under who reported only one type of kindred in their pool of relatives.

Sixty-five percent of the respondents 65 years old and over with one type of kindred available reported only joint descendants in their pool of relatives.

The possibility that there are shifts in recruitment from one type of kindred to another among respondents at different age levels—in particular the possibility that older people might be more involved with their close kindred than with joint descendants—must be put in proper light in view of the negative associations between age and the availability of kindreds. Not only do fewer older respondents with kin in the metropolitan area report any representatives of close, spouse's, and distant kindred available, but those who do report them generally have fewer representatives of that kindred type available to them than do younger respondents. Thus if there is a general shift in recruitment of any of these kindred such that older people utilize this opportunity structure more fully, it will hold for a smaller number of respondents, and such relationships could occur with fewer representatives of these kindred. And for many older people, the possibility of solidarity with collaterals simply does not exist.

Since we have found (Chapter 3) that the number of representatives of close, spouse's, and distant kindred available to an individual is an important consideration in whether any are seen, we will have to examine closely the possible differential bearing this dimension of the opportunity structure of kindreds may have on the recruitment of kin among respondents at different age levels. For example, while proportionately fewer older respondents may see any representatives of close kindred available to them, they may in fact utilize this opportunity structure more fully than younger respondents. These issues will be examined later in this chapter.

However, let us now look at the relation between marital status and the availability of close and spouse's kindreds. The majority (70 percent) of the 1,434 respondents with kin in the metropolitan area were married at the time of the interview. Some individuals (5 percent), however, never married, while for others (4.5 percent) marriage was disrupted through separation or divorce, and for still others (21 percent) through the death of a spouse.

Regardless of age, married respondents have more types of kindred available to them than those not married at the time of the interview because kinship roles found in spouse's kindred and joint descendant kindred do not exist for those who never married. However, the fact that respondents whose marriage was *disrupted* have fewer types of kindred available to them than those who were married bears close examination, as kinship roles found in joint descendant kindred and one's spouse's kindred do exist for these respondents.

The disruption of marriage through divorce, separation, or the death of one's spouse, however, raises special problems. There is some question whether the disruption of marriage may entail migration to be nearer one's own close kindred. Also of particular interest are the possible consequences of the disruption of the conjugal relationship on an individual's relationship with his former spouse's kindred. If the disruption of marriage entails a migration to close kindred, fewer respondents who are married as compared to those no longer married might report close kindred in the area. The pertinent evidence is found in the Total row of Table 4-2. (Respondents who never married are omitted from this table since they are not germane to the question at hand.)

There is little difference by marital status in the proportion of respondents who reported close kindred among their pool of relatives, as the Total row shows. However, there is a large difference by marital status in whether spouse's kindred are represented. For only 23 percent of respondents who are no longer married report representatives of their former spouse's kindred in the pool of relatives. But over half the married respondents report spouse's kindred available. It is probable that respondents no longer married do not recognize as kin their former spouse's kindred.

The cells of Table 4-2 permit a further examination of this relationship, holding age constant. There remain negligible differences, in proportions of respondents reporting close kindred, between those whose marriages have been disrupted and the presently married. When age is held constant, present marital status makes little difference in whether or not close kindred are available. However it makes a very considerable difference where spouse's kindred are concerned. At each age level, when those presently married are compared with those whose marriages have been disrupted, about twice as large a proportion of the former report spouse's kindred available. So regardless of age, spouse's kindred are not reported as represented to any great extent in the pool of relatives of those no longer married. Moreover, the reason why the respondent is no longer married is also important. More widows (24 percent) report spouse's

Table 4-2
Respondents Who Reported Available Close and Spouse's Kindred
in the Pool of Available Relatives by Age and Marital Status
(In Percentages)

	Close Kindred		Spouse's Kindred	
Age	Presently Married	Marriage Disrupted	Presently Married	Marriage Disrupted
65 and over	51.8 (351)	49.3 (201)	43.9 (351)	20.4 (201)
55-64	66.0 (297)	72.4 (105)	53.9 (297)	27.6 (105)
54 and under	79.3 (352)	72.2 (54)	66.2 (352)	25.9 (54)
Total	65.7 (1,000)	59.4 (360)	54.7 (1,000)	23.3 (360)
Gamma	−.405	−.427	−.303	−.146

kindred available to them than respondents who were separated or divorced (18 percent). Holding age constant does not alter this pattern.

The clue to the association between marital status and reporting spouse's kindred in the metropolitan area lies in the nature of our kinship system considered from a cultural standpoint. Essentially, there is some question whether an individual whose marriage was disrupted will even consider his former spouse's kindred as relatives, and, if he does, whether any relationships with them are maintained. This is Schneider's (1968:92) viewpoint, as discussed above.

While such a perspective may be true for our respondents' relationships with their former spouse's kindred, it should not affect the geographical availability of such kin unless the disruption of marriage resulted in a move on the part of the respondent. But by and large this is a geographically stable sample. Over 50 percent of these working class people have lived in metropolitan Philadelphia all their lives, and among these people native to the Philadelphia area, the association between marital status and reporting spouse's kindred in the area remains. Over 60 percent of those who were married and who lived in metropolitan Philadelphia all their lives reported representatives of spouse's kindred in their pool of relatives, while less than 30 percent of those whose marriage was disrupted and who lived in the area all of their lives reported spouse's kindred available.

These findings indicate that whether spouse's kindred are or are not objectively available, subjectively at least they are not defined in the pool of relatives of respondents who are no longer married. As we noted in an earlier chapter, the definition of who one's relatives are was not left to the respondent's recognition of kin. Information was gathered about the genealogically possible pool of relatives, who were enumerated on the interview schedule. Moreover, the relatives who are reported are not kin the respondents knew only vaguely; each of the respondents was questioned about each relative he reported and the respondent had to know each relative's name and where he lived for that relative to be included in the study. The data we do have indicate that respondents refused, when questioned, to recognize the spouse's kindred as relatives, or the respondents lost contact with these relatives to the extent they did not remember their names or where they lived. The reason that fewer divorced and separated (compared to widows) reported spouse's kindred seems to lie in the basis on which marriage was terminated—purposeful versus involuntary. Some differential cultural sanctions would appear to attach to these different forms of nuptual termination.

In any case, for this working class sample, whether marriage is terminated through divorce or separation or the death of a spouse, representatives of one's former spouse's kindred are no longer counted in the pool of relatives of many people. From the point of view of the working class person himself, occupants of kinship roles previously recognized as relatives become nonkin by default, as it were. While it is true that working class people who are no longer married omit spouse's kindred from their pool of relatives, there is no evidence that the disruption of their marriages resulted in a turn (or return) to their own close kindred. For marital status appears to be unrelated to their geographical movements. And those who do not move still manifest the pattern of association reported above. Thus, even among those respondents who lived in the area all of their lives, there are major differences by marital status in whether spouse's kindred are available.

Interaction and Age

With the interrelations of age, marital status, and availability of kindreds in mind, we turn to kinship interaction. In this section we will examine patterns of interaction with all four types of kindred by age of respondent. Here we will attempt to discover whether the aged are the focal figures of urban kinship relations, and whether specific types of kindred are more likely to be seen by older respondents than by younger respondents. In the next section of this chapter we will examine patterns of interaction with close and spouse's kindred by age and present marital status simultaneously. It will be recalled that the role composition of these two kindred types is similar with the exception that close kindred are related to the respondent while spouse's kindred are the respondent's inlaws. We will want to know whether there are differences by present marital status in the interaction of our respondents with these two distinct types of kindred, and whether the association between age and recruitment of these kindred is different for the married and those who are not presently married.

First, we examine age differences in recruitment of kindred for interaction. The minimal condition which must be met by older people in order to be considered the focal points of kinship interaction is that they see as many or more types of kindred as younger people. Are there, then, differences by age in the number of types of kindred seen? In answering this question we shall control for the number of types of kindred available since, as we just saw, age is negatively associated with the number of types of kindred in this sample's pool of relatives. If older respondents are the foci of kin relations in the sense that they have contact with more types of kindred, one would expect that more older people would see all types of kindred available to them than younger respondents. And in addition we would also expect that a larger proportion of available kindred types would be seen by older than younger respondents. The relevant data are presented in Tables 4-3 and 4-4.

Table 4-3 shows the relation between age and interaction with all available types of kindred. This table reveals that with one exception fewer older respondents than younger respondents were in contact with all types of kindred available to them. With the exception of respondents for whom only one type of

Table 4-3

Respondents Who Saw All Available Kindred Types, by Age and Number of Kindred Types Available (In Percentages)

Age	Number of Kindred Types Available			
	One	Two	Three	Four
65 and over	65.6	37.6	15.9	15.9
	(198)	(206)	(132)	(44)
55-64	71.8	43.7	28.8	15.9
	(117)	(119)	(118)	(69)
54 and under	59.5	43.7	43.0	25.0
	(89)	(135)	(151)	(56)

Table 4-4

Proportion of Available Kindred Types Seen, by Age (In Percentages)

Age	Number of Kindred Types Available			
	One	Two	Three	Four
65 and over	65.6	47.4	51.5	62.8
	(198)	(206)	(132)	(44)
55-64	71.8	63.8	59.9	60.1
	(117)	(119)	(118)	(69)
54 and under	59.5	62.9	69.5	67.9
	(89)	(135)	(151)	(56)

kindred was available, age is inversely related to total integration with available kindred types. This inverse relationship suggests that older people are not the foci of kinship relations; and it would seem to indicate that older people might be more selective than younger people in the types of kindred they contact.

Table 4-4 shows the relationship between age and the proportion of available kindred seen. (The proportion of available kindreds seen was calculated by the procedure discussed in Chapter 3.) The upper right hand cell of this table, for example, should be read as follows: 62.8 percent, on the average, of the available kindred types were contacted by the 44 respondents age 65 and over who had all four kindred types available to them. It should be understood that it is not the number of representatives of a given kindred type or types which are represented in these figures. Rather, they show what proportion of people saw the full variety of available types of kindred, and conversely what proportion saw kin belonging to only some but not all of the available kindred types. Thus Table 4-4 is evidence that the aged are not the central figures in the relational system of kinship any more than are the younger people.

The proportion of available kindred types seen by older respondents is generally not larger than the proportion seen by younger respondents. Among those with two or more types of kindred available, older respondents see proportionately fewer of the available kindred types than younger respondents. Hence, as the range of choice available to older people expands to two, three, and four types of kindred the proportion who take advantage of these larger opportunities for kin contact by seeing someone from every available type of kin never exceeds the proportion of younger people, age 54 and under, who do so. Apparently old people are more selective than younger people in terms of the variety of relatives seen.

Thus we find no support for the thesis that the aged are the foci of kin relations. Even in the exceptional and restrictive case where younger people are less integrated into their network of kin (that is, when only one type of kindred is available), it is the 55- to 64-year-olds rather than those 65 and over who are more involved with their relatives—as can be seen in Tables 4-3 and 4-4. What are the underlying reasons why fewer older respondents see all types of kindred available and proportionately fewer available types are seen by them? Does age affect the recruitment of each type of kindred in the same way? In other words, how much flexibility is there in the structure of the relational system of kinship? Are there shifts in the type of kindred recruited from one age level to another which are hidden by these findings which deal only with number and variety of kindred types? Or is it the case that older people are less likely to see any and all types of kindred available? The association between age and contact with close kindred is of particular concern to us in this connection. Do more older than younger respondents see these collaterals (who are the bulk of this sample's close kindred), as Cumming and Schneider suggest, or is contact with them attenuated with age, as Young and Wilmott suggest? We gain initial insight into these matters by examining whether there are differences in the number of respondents at each age level who saw one or more representatives of the specific types of kindred available to them.

Table 4-5 shows the number of respondents at each age level who recruited each of the specific types of kindred represented in their pool of relatives. (The number appearing in parenthesis in each cell is the number of respondents reporting representatives of that kindred available and is the base upon which the percentages who saw them were computed.) The pattern of older respondents not seeing as many types of kindred as the younger people, which was revealed in Tables 4-3 and 4-4, results—as we see in Table 4-5—from fewer older than younger people seeing their close, spouse's, and distant kindred. For about as many older as younger people saw their joint descendants; thus age is inversely associated with seeing close, spouse's, and distant kindred as the Gamma's in Table 4-5 reveal. But, as these measures indicate, the relation of age and contact with close kindred is stronger than the associations of age and contact with spouse's and distant kindred.

Table 4-5
Respondents Who Saw Specific Kindred Types, by Age
(In Percentages)

Age	Close Kindred	Spouse's Kindred	Distant Kindred	Joint Descendant Kindred
65 and over	45.7	47.2	35.3	86.5
	(304)	(195)	(289)	(394)
55-64	59.7	50.8	45.7	90.6
	(288)	(189)	(254)	(254)
54 and under	74.0	65.2	53.2	82.0
	(342)	(247)	(314)	(133)
Gamma:	−.389	−.253	−.244	+.031

While we do not infer a longitudinal trend from a cross-sectional measure, nevertheless, unless there are generational cohort effects of unprecedented magnitude in our data, the negative association between age and contact with close kindred would seem to lend support to Young and Wilmott's view that relationships with these kin become attenuated in later stages of life. There is no indication of marked "solidarity" of older people with close kindred (which is composed of siblings mainly) for the sample as a whole.

The fact that older as compared to younger respondents did not interact with as many types of available kindred is thus a consequence of fewer older respondents seeing specific types of kindred: close, spouse's, and distant. Moreover, these data do not indicate that there are shifts from recruitment of one type of kindred to another with increasing age. In Table 4-5 we see that the rank order of specific kindred types seen remains constant at each age level: the highest proportion of respondents saw available joint descendants, while the lowest proportion saw distant kindred when they were available. The proportion of respondents who saw close kindred and spouse's kindred fall between these two extremes.

Consonant with the preceding findings, these negative associations between age and contact with close, distant, and spouse's kindred do not support the theory that the aged are the foci of urban kin relations or that there is an emphasis on the solidarity of older respondents with their close kindred (siblings). However, we previously found that age is inversely related to the number of representatives of these kindred which are available. Since the number of representatives of close, distant, and spouse's kindred available to the sample is associated with whether any representatives of that kindred are seen, the question does arise as to whether the inverse relationships we have found in Table 4-5 are due to individual factors that promote social isolation in the aged person or whether they are due to the diminished number of representatives of these kindred which are available at late ages. The relationships shown in Table 4-5 could have come about for either or both of these reasons. Are there differences by age in the utilization of the available opportunity structures of kindreds?

In order to answer this question we will again examine the mean number of kin seen and the mean frequency of contact with kindred available to respondents at different age levels. We noted in Chapter 3 that these aspects of kinship interaction can be presented by an index having the property of statistically reducing the number of representatives of a kindred available to the base of one. If the utilization of the opportunity structures of available kindred is different for older and younger people, then the mean number of available representatives of a kindred seen will vary with age, since the size of the opportunity structure is controlled in this measure. The mean number of contacts with available kindred will also vary with age for the same reason. On the other hand, if the differences in patterns of recruitment of available kindreds are due to the size of the opportunity structures of each kindred, there will be no differences by age in these two measures of recruitment of a specific kindred. In the former case we may presume that age itself or age-related factors contribute in some measure to these aspects of kinship interaction, while in the latter case it is probable that abundance or scarcity of relatives in the local area is an important element in the amount of contact a person has with kin.

The mean number of kin seen and the frequency of contact index for each kindred type are shown in Table 4-6. The scores arrayed in this table for each age category were obtained by the procedure described in Chapter 3. As can be seen from the table, there are differences in the scope and extent of recruitment of kindreds by age. Therefore, interaction with specific types of kindred is not contextually determined by the number of available representatives of these kindred types. In addition, the extent of the differences depends upon the type of kindred and which measure of recruitment of kin for interaction is used. The most important differences by age occur in the recruitment of close kindred: there are considerable differences in both the mean number of close kindred seen and the mean frequency of interaction.

As we found above in Table 4-5, age is strongly associated with recruitment of close kindred. Having controlled in Table 4-6 for the number of representatives of those kindred available, we see that the inverse relation between age and the utilization of the opportunity structures of these kindred remains similar to the pattern reported in Table 4-5. Thus the findings in Table 4-6 indicate that the differences in the number of representatives of a kindred available to respondents at different ages do not distort the associations by age, when we use as indices the mean number of these kindred seen and the mean frequency of contacts.

The inverse associations between age and the mean number of available close kindred seen, and between age and the mean frequency of interaction with close

Table 4-6
Extent and Frequency of Contact with Specific Kindred Types by Age of Respondents

Age	Close Kindred			Spouse's Kindred			Distant Kindred			Joint Descendant Kindred		
	Mean Number Seen[a]	Mean Frequency of Contact[b]	(N)	Mean Number Seen	Mean Frequency of Contact	(N)	Mean Number Seen	Mean Frequency of Contact	(N)	Mean Number Seen	Mean Frequency of Contact	(N)
65 and over	.34	.65	(305)	.35	.71	(195)	.17	.47	(289)	.66	1.66	(394)
55-64	.42	.78	(288)	.36	.63	(189)	.29	.62	(254)	.76	2.56	(254)
54 and under	.51	1.08	(342)	.39	.76	(247)	.30	.59	(314)	.74	2.25	(133)

[a]Range: 0-1
[b]Range: 0-7

kindred contradict Cumming and Schneider's (1961) view that relatives comprising this kindred (specifically siblings) increasingly become axes along which social interaction occurs in the later years of life. For interaction patterns with relatives comprising close kindred are attenuated among older respondents. Older respondents saw or contacted fewer of the close kindred available to them than did younger respondents. The major differences occur in frequency of interaction. Close kindred of the younger respondents were contacted almost twice as often as were close kindred of respondents 65 years and over, controlling for the effects of the number of close kindred who are available.

In comparison with close kindred, the recruitment of other types of available kindred is not as strongly associated with age. (However the differences by age that do occur bear examination.) The utilization of the opportunity structure of spouse's kindred is least associated with age of respondent. There are but minor differences in the mean number of available spouse's kindred seen and mean frequency of contacts with spouse's kindred among respondents at different ages. (The question of whether this pattern holds equally for married and those no longer married and for husbands and wives will be examined later in this chapter and in the next chapter.)

Also consistent with the information presented in Table 4-5, we see in Table 4-6 that age is inversely related to recruitment of distant kindred. The major differences occur between older respondents (65 and over) and the remaining younger members of the sample. Interaction with distant kindred is attenuated among these older respondents. Fewer of those distant kindred who were available to respondents 65 and over were seen, and the interaction that occurred was infrequent. Older respondents simply do not utilize the available opportunity structure of distant kindred to an appreciable degree.

In Table 4-5 we found that age of respondents was not strongly associated with whether any contacts occurred with joint descendants. A majority of respondents at each age level saw these relatives. However, the findings reported in Table 4-6 indicate that there is a negative association between age and the frequency of contacts with joint descendant kindred. The major differences are between the oldest (65 and over) and the rest of the respondents. Interaction with joint descendant kindred available to the older respondents is also attenuated in the sense that the mean number of available joint descendant kindred seen is somewhat lower for respondents 65 and over, however it is plain that the differences in frequency of contact are more important. For mean frequency of contact with joint descendant kindred available to younger respondents is about one and one-half times larger than that of older respondents, whereas the decline in mean number of joint descendants seen is slight. These measures indicate that while the available number of joint descendants seen remains fairly constant or declines somewhat, the frequency with which those joint descendants who are seen are contacted by older respondents is less. Thus social relationships with joint descendants are maintained throughout life, but the level of interaction with these relatives becomes attenuated in the later stages of the life cycle.

Table 4-6 permits us to give a tentative answer to the question of whether there are shifts from one type of kindred to another in the utilization of the opportunity structure of kin by respondents at different ages. Is one type of kindred favored for interaction among younger respondents while another is favored among older respondents? Judging from this evidence there are no apparent shifts by age from recruitment of one type of kindred to another. Within each age level the rank order, across different kindred types, of mean frequency of contact and mean number of relatives seen remains fairly constant. In comparison with the other types of kindred, opportunity structure of distant kindred are least utilized by respondents within each age level. The pool of joint descendants in the local area is the most fully utilized opportunity structure.

Within each age level the utilization of the opportunity structures of close and spouse's kindred fall between these two extremes of distant and joint descendant kindred. Thus the basic structure of the relational system remains intact among respondents at different ages, as evidenced by the absence of any apparent shifts in the pattern of interaction from one type of kindred to another. And at the same time we can see the specific effect of age, namely, a lessening utilization of the opportunity structure of close, distant, and joint descendant kindred (bilateral kindred) among older respondents.

Our data thus lend support to the view that the negative associations between age and contact with kindred are due to factors that promote isolation in the aged person and not to the diminished number of representatives of those kindred available at late ages. In light of evidence presented in Chapter 3 on the inverse relation between contact with kindred and geographical distance, the question does arise whether the explanation for the relative isolation of the aged is due to fewer older people having relatives living nearby. That is, is isolation promoted by the ecology of kin dispersion, which, as well as size, is a characteristic of the opportunity structure? If isolation from kin among older people is primarily a function of the ecological distribution of relatives, then the negative association between age and contact with kindred should disappear when geographical distance is held constant. The proportion of respondents who saw specific kindred by age, holding geographical distance constant, is presented in Table 4-7.

Table 4-7 shows that the relative isolation of the aged from contacts with close, spouse's, and distant kindred is not due to the ecology of kin dispersion. That is, age is negatively associated with contacts with close, spouse's, and distant kindred when these relatives live within six blocks of our respondents as well as when they live six or more blocks away. While it is the case that older people are less likely than younger people to have kindred living nearby (see numbers appearing in parenthesis in Table 4-7), those older people who have such kindred living within six blocks of their homes still are less likely to see them than are younger respondents.

Table 4-7
Respondents Who Saw Available Kindred Types, by Age
and Geographical Distance (In Percentages)

Age	Geographical Distance	Close Kindred	Spouse's Kindred	Distant Kindred	Joint Descendant Kindred
65 and over	Within six blocks	66.2 (68)	76.3 (38)	55.9 (59)	96.4 (138)
	Six blocks or more	40.0 (270)	38.8 (170)	31.4 (255)	80.5 (343)
55-64	Within six blocks	75.3 (81)	55.8 (43)	63.6 (77)	97.5 (81)
	Six blocks or more	51.0 (255)	47.3 (169)	36.2 (221)	86.1 (209)
54 and under	Within six blocks	85.5 (110)	79.7 (79)	71.2 (111)	90.6 (32)
	Six blocks or more	64.3 (308)	55.3 (217)	41.5 (282)	80.7 (114)
Gamma:	Within six blocks	−.354	−.172	−.219	+.203
	Six blocks or more	−.325	−.222	−.150	+.073

However, joint descendant kin are something of an exception, since those who live close by are seen by a slightly larger proportion of our older than younger respondents, while those who live farther away are seen by about the same proportion of older as younger people. But the differences in the percentages are quite small—on the order of six or seven percentage points—and the relationship between age and contact is curvilinear moreover. So at the most, older people see their joint descendant kin at about the same rate as younger people, but they can hardly be said to see them in larger proportions than do younger people.

Interaction and Marital Status

At this juncture we introduce an additional consideration that may shed more light on the relation of age to patterns of recruitment of close and spouse's kindred: present marital status. Does the presence or absence of a spouse influence the recruitment of close and spouse's kindred? While there is agreement that the conjugal relation is important in comparison with other kinship bonds, little is known about how the absence of such a relationship affects patterns of recruitment of close and spouse's kindred. Cumming and

Schneider (1961:502) note, although they present no evidence to support their contention, that the shifts in solidarity through time to an emphasis on siblings is partly a characteristic of the stage of family development. Cumming and Schneider do not state specifically whether they are referring to the presence or absence of the spouse. We have presented some evidence (Table 4-3) that indicates that when the spouse is not present, relationships with spouse's kindred might be attenuated. Compared to the married respondents, 36 percent fewer respondents who are no longer married reported spouse's kindred in their pool of relatives.

In view of these considerations, we ask the following questions: Does the negative association between age and the recruitment of close and spouse's kindred hold equally for those who are and who are not presently married?[a] And, are available close and spouse's kindred contacted equally as often by those presently married and unmarried?

Table 4-8 shows the relation of marital status and age to interaction with close and spouse's kindred. These data indicate that there are substantial differences by our respondent's age and present marital status in whether interaction occurs with close and spouse's kindred. For close kindred, the association between age and interaction is negative and is higher for the presently married (Gamma: $-.463$) than for the not presently married (Gamma: $-.178$). Thus Table 4-8 reveals that it is among the married that strong attenuation of contacts with close kindred occur with age. But still, within each age level it is the unmarried who see close kindred in larger proportions (with the exception of those respondents who were 54 and under, where there is virtually no difference between the proportion of married and unmarried who saw available close kindred). Perhaps these relatives serve compensatory functions for the unmarried.

In the case of spouse's kindred, the association between age and interaction is negative and stronger for those presently married (Gamma: $-.273$) than those not presently married (Gamma: $+.069$). But this pattern of interaction with spouse's kindred has a different meaning from the one we observed for close kindred. That is the role of the respondent's marital status differs depending on which kindred type, close or spouse's, is being recruited. For one, we have in these figures the imponderable influence of the nonreporting or nonrecognition of spouse's kindred (which we mentioned earlier) on the part of those not presently married. A glance at Table 4-8 reveals, where spouse's kindred are concerned, that proportionately more married than unmarried people interact with these relatives; and there is a small increase in this proportion by age among the unmarried and a substantial decline among the married.

[a]Not presently married includes those who are widows (71%), divorced or separated (13%), and never married (16%). Of those not presently, but who at one time had been, married, 19 percent reported spouse's kindred in the metropolitan area. Most unmarried respondents who did report spouse's kindred available were widows (88%).

Table 4-8
Respondents Who Saw Close Kindred and Spouse's Kindred,
by Age and Present Marital Status (In Percentages)

Age	Present Marital Status	Close Kindred	Spouse's Kindred
65 and over	Married	40.1 (182)	48.7 (154)
	Not married	54.1 (122)	41.5 (41)
55-64	Married	56.6 (196)	51.2 (160)
	Not married	66.3 (92)	48.3 (29)
54 and under	Married	74.5 (279)	67.4 (233)
	Not married	71.4 (63)	28.6 (14)
Total	Married	59.7 (657)	57.4 (547)
	Not married	62.1 (277)	41.7 (84)[a]
Gamma:	Married	−.463	−.273
	Not married	−.178	+.069

[a]Never married respondents excluded.

By contrast we just saw that proportionately fewer married than not married people interact with close kindred, and that the decline in interaction with age is much steeper for the married. Furthermore, reading across the columns of Table 4-8 and comparing the proportions of people in each marital status (either in the totals or by age levels) who interact with close and spouse's kindred, we observe that the dissolution of the marital bond has most likely also dissolved the equalitarian emphasis in recruitment of kin. For among unmarried respondents of any age, proportionately fewer of them see their former spouse's kindred than their close kindred—while among married people there is hardly any difference in these proportions.

This also suggests that in the absence of the conjugal relation there is an attempt to maintain social relationships with close kindred, especially since contacts with close kindred among married respondents become attenuated more sharply among old people who are married than among those who are not. The absence of the spouse who may initiate such activities with his or her own kindred is an obvious factor involved in the lack of contact with spouse's kindred among those no longer married. What might be considered equalitarian treatment of one's own kindred and one's spouse's kindred for purposes of interaction holds only as long as the conjugal relationship is intact.

Thus far we have found differences by age and marital status in sheer contact with close and spouse's kindred. We turn now to the parallel analysis of differences by age and marital status in the mean number of close kindred and spouse's kindred seen and the mean frequency of contact with them. The data are presented in Table 4-9.

Considering close kindred first, the negative association between age and interaction which we saw in Table 4-8 is maintained here for both married and unmarried people, and, as in Table 4-8, is stronger for married respondents. Specifically, married respondents 54 years and under see a mean number of close kindred which is about one and one-half times larger than the corresponding figure for married respondents 65 and over. Also, the mean frequency of interaction with close kindred is about twice as large for these younger respondents than older respondents. But people who are not presently married, and 54 and under, see a mean number of close kindred which is only about a tenth larger than not-married people 65 and over. And the mean frequency of interaction with close kindred is only about half as large for these younger unmarried people than for the older unmarried people.

Still parallel to the findings of Table 4-8, Table 4-9 shows that it is those who are not presently married who recruit more close kindred and who see them more often. The data show, within each age category, the mean number of close kindred seen and the mean frequency of interaction with close kindred is larger for not married than married respondents.

Turning to spouse's kindred, the mean number of kin seen and the mean frequency of contact with available kindred is not so strongly associated with

Table 4-9
Extent and Frequency of Contact with Close Kindred and Spouse's Kindred, by Age and Marital Status

| Age | Present Marital Status | Close Kindred | | | Spouse's Kindred | | |
		Mean Number Seen[a]	Mean Frequency of Contact[b]	(N)	Mean Number Seen	Mean Frequency of Contact	(N)
65 and over	Married	.29	.49	(182)	.36	.56	(154)
	Not married	.48	.89	(122)	.37	.64	(41)
55-64	Married	.40	.73	(196)	.37	.63	(160)
	Not married	.45	1.46	(92)	.34	.52	(29)
54 and under	Married	.51	1.03	(279)	.47	.80	(233)
	Not married	.53	1.35	(63)	.13	.15	(14)

[a]Range: 0-1
[b]Range: 0-7

age. For people who are not married the association is, in addition to being weaker than what we found for close kindred, positive rather than negative. Again, this is the pattern of relationships we observed in Table 4-8, where we were considering only the proportions of respondents who contacted these relatives. However, as opposed to what we found for close kindred, for those under age 65 it is not the case that the married recruit fewer spouse's kindred and see them less frequently; rather, the opposite is true. Even among those 65 years and over, the differences by marital status are small. But it must be pointed out again that the findings on utilization of the opportunity structure of spouse's kindred by respondents not presently married should be viewed with caution.

Despite the tentative interpretation that should be made of recruitment of former spouse's kindred among not married respondents, we can look at the question of whether close and spouse's kindred who are available to married and not married people are treated equally in interaction. Table 4-9 shows that among people who are no longer married, the opportunity structure of close kindred is utilized more fully than the opportunity structure of spouse's kindred. Thus for whatever reason, and regardless of age, these unmarried people do not treat close kindred and (former) spouse's kindred equally. Representatives of former spouse's kindred are neither seen by the unmarried in as great number nor contacted as often as close kindred.

Compared to these patterns of interaction with close and spouse's kindred by the unmarried, married people do treat representatives of these kindred relatively more equally in general. However, there are some minor differences which depend on the ages of the married respondents, and which have to do with frequency of interaction. That is, younger married people, especially those under age 55, interact less frequently with their spouse's kindred than with close kindred. But again, the major point is still that spouse's kindred and close kindred for the most part are treated equally as long as the conjugal relation is intact.

Conclusion

At the beginning of this chapter, we raised the question of how factors associated with the life cycle are related to the principle of selection of kin for interaction. We have seen, generally speaking, that the age and marital status of a working class person has a bearing on which of his available relatives will be seen, the number of such kin seen, and the frequency of interaction with these kin. But the specific way in which these variables are related to recruitment of relatives depends on the type of kindred in question. This can be seen best by looking back at some of the substantive issues of the chapter.

We asked whether the aged were central figures in the relational system of kinship and whether that system was flexible over the life cycle, so that the patterned order of kinship interaction we observed in the preceding chapter is preserved at all ages. Concerning the role of the aged, we found that, consistent with the argument of Chapter 1 that kinship relations in our society are primarily ego-focused, old people are not central figures in kinship interaction in the working class. Our findings do not support Adams's view that the aged are the foci of urban kin relations. Age is inversely associated with having any contact with three of the four types of kindred, joint descendants being somewhat of an exception. Moreover, the opportunity structure of available kindred is less fully utilized by older than by younger respondents. However, this also depends on the type of kindred in question and whether we are examining the number of relatives contacted or the frequency of contact. For example, age has little to do with the number of joint descendants contacted, but on the other hand older people do interact less frequently with these relatives than do younger respondents.

While the opportunity structure of joint descendant kindred is most fully utilized for purposes of interaction regardless of the respondent's age, that of distant kindred is least utilized by all respondents. While age is negatively associated with the number of distant kindred contacted, age has less of a bearing on the frequency of contacts with these kindred. While fewer distant kindred are seen by older respondents than younger respondents, the frequency of interaction with available distant kindred is as high for older as for younger respondents.

In addition, our findings do not provide conclusive support for Cumming and Schneider's view that representatives of close kindred become important sources of socioemotional interaction in later stages of life but they do support Young and Wilmott's view that relationships with these kin generally become attenuated in later stages of life. However, none of these authors saw that the presence or absence of the conjugal relationships plays a crucial role in interaction patterns with close kindred. The question of the extent to which contacts with close kindred are attenuated with age depends on marital status, for age bears a stronger negative association on all three dimensions of interaction with close kindred among married respondents than among respondents who are not married.

The normative pattern of treating close and spouse's kindred equally is reflected in patterns of interaction as long as the marriage is intact. But upon the disruption of marriage, one's former spouse's kindred are not subjectively considered as kin by most respondents. Those respondents who do recognize former spouse's kindred as relatives either do not see them at all or else they see such kin quite frequently. The pattern of interaction with former spouse's kindred is one characterized by a great deal of variability. However, coupled with this variability in recognition and contact with former spouse's kindred is the pattern of entrenched interaction with close kindred for these presently unmarried people. In the absence of the conjugal bond, close kindred are seen.

Since we do not have longitudinal data, we cannot tell definitely whether the disruption of the conjugal relation entails an attempt to re-establish affective bonds with the remaining representatives of one's close kindred. But since the disruption of marriage is associated with the attenuation of relationships with one's former spouse's kindred and since not being married is associated with greater utilization of the opportunity structure of one's close kindred, these findings indicate that the minimal condition for one's own kindred to be an important source—in this context—of socioemotional interaction have been met.

We have also shown that the pattern of kinship interaction identified in the previous chapter is flexible enough to persist through the changes and vicissitudes of the life cycle. At all ages, and regardless of geographical distance between our respondents and their kin, and regardless of the dimension of interaction measured, and controlling for availability, joint descendant kindred are seen most, distant kindred least, and close and spouse's kindred about equally and in between the other two. Thus we have found, as in the preceding chapter, that age is a variable resembling geographical distance in the sense that it is responsible for some of the variability in kinship relations yet at the same time does not disrupt the patterned order of the kindred-based linkage system of interaction.

5 Matricentricity

It is our contention in this chapter that in a kinship system such as our own, both the husband and the wife act as pivotal links in maintaining relationships with their respective kindred. Turner (1968:29) is among the few who have espoused this view, and for English kinship systems moreover. In this view, if either the husband or wife is unable or unwilling to maintain social relationships with his or her kindred, then relationships with these kindred will be minimized for the conjugal pair. The important role that the husband or wife plays in maintaining ties with his or her own kindred was clearly demonstrated in the preceding chapter where we found that relationships with one's spouse's kindred are attenuated upon the termination of the marriage.

Although there is a normative pattern specifying equalitarian treatment of the kindred of each spouse in recruitment for interaction, there may be variability in the extent to which this prescript is realized in fact. And as we shall see shortly, many have erroneously seized upon this variability in proposing the thesis of matricentricity. In this chapter, then, we will examine whether there are husband-wife differences in the utilization of the available opportunity structure of the husband's and the wife's close kindred and the extent to which these husbands or wives are pulled into the social arena of their respective spouse's kindred. Of particular concern is whether the husbands and wives comprising our sample act as links for their spouses in interaction with their respective close kindred. Also, we will examine whether any characteristic of these respondents and of their conjugal relationship provide clarification of the kinship relations which we do find.

Several issues in the kinship literature, as well as the findings in the previous chapter, have a bearing on the problem addressed in this chapter; we will examine these first.

The Matricentricity Hypothesis and Related Issues

Most studies of urban kinship focus on social relationships which occur between the sampled respondents and their own bilateral kindred. Relatively few studies have examined relationships between the respondents and spouse's kindred and even fewer have examined husband-wife differences in interaction with kindred. We are, therefore, working in a largely unknown area. However, three issues in the kinship literature do have a particular bearing on the problem of husband-wife differences in interaction with kindred: (1) female involvement with kin; (2) the "matricentric" or "matrilateral" bias; and (3) characteristics of the conjugal relationship. They will be discussed briefly in turn.

It is not frequent that there is consensus in a body of social science literature over a particular issue. This happens to be the case, however, over sex differences in relationships with kin. Adams (1968:4), in summarizing a number of studies, claims that "females are more involved in kin affairs than men. They bear the major burden of the general obligation of keeping in touch with kin." According to Robins and Tomanec (1962:345), women tend to act as representatives of the nuclear family (i.e., domestic unit) in fulfilling obligations to kin.

Since women fulfill obligations to kin, this means that upon marriage a woman's kinship duties are expanded to include her husband's kindred. It follows that it is the wife's duty to maintain equal contacts with both kindreds. There is some indication, however, that there is a difference by socioeconomic status in the extent to which this duty is put into practice. Adams (1968:169-170) found that middle class wives in his sample maintain contacts with both their own and their husband's parents when they were geographically distant; however, working class wives concentrated on their own parents to the neglect of their husband's parents when both were geographically distant.

A few studies of working class kinship relations (Young and Wilmott, 1957; Komarovsky, 1962) have found that more wives maintain contact with all representatives of their close kindred than either they or their husbands maintain contact with his own kindred. These studies suggest that working class men are pulled into the social arena of their inlaws to the partial neglect of their own kindred.

The tendency—especially among working class people—to limit interaction to the wife's kindred has been variously referred to as: "asymmetrical kinship" (Farber); a "matricentric bias" (Komarovsky); a "matrilateral bias" (Bott); "matrilaterality" (Coult and Habenstein); and so on. The use of such neologisms while implying that there is an openness about our kinship system which permits either spouse's kindred to be favored over the other also assumes that social relationships are particularly stressed in the female's line of descent.[a] While on the one hand the concepts used to explain the female's involvement with her kindred suggest that it has something to do with characteristics of our kinship system, nevertheless, on the other hand, the explanations offered are largely based on other factors. Of particular concern are those explanations based on differential residential patterns, cultural differences in the definition of sex roles, and characteristics of the conjugal relation.

[a]In the anthropological kinship literature, the term "matricentricity" is used to refer to a family form where the female turns to her kin when the husband is unable to perform his economic role. According to Mogey (1964:514) such unstable conjugal bonds have been reported among lower-lower class whites in the United States. However when we examined differences in interaction patterns with respective kindreds of husband and wife among the poor and modest income families in this study we found no differences by income status in contacts with the kindred of the husband or the wife.

One aspect of the matricentricity issue rests on the alleged tendency of working class people to reside in the neighborhood of the wife and the wife's relatives. For example, studies of British working class families find that husbands generally come to reside in the neighborhood of the wife and her kin (Mogey, 1964; Young and Wilmott, 1957). The explanation of the greater involvement of husband and wife with the wife's kindred thus rests on differences in geographical distance between married couples and their respective kindred.

We take the position that the question of differentials in the geographical dispersion of the husband's kindred as compared to those of the wife is an empirical one. And, the issue of favoring the wife's kindred over the husband's would have to be examined in light of these differentials. Data on kinship relations in the United States do not show a matrifocal tendency, and we simply do not know whether matrifocality alone produces matricentricity or whether other factors are involved as well.

One such explanation for the greater involvement of females with kin has as its major theoretical rationale cultural differences in the definitions of sex roles. Despite the "emancipation" of women, the woman's role continues to revolve primarily around domestic tasks. As Mirande notes (1968:156) one consequence of this domestic orientation is that wives are more active than their husbands in maintaining ties with kin.

While this rationale might explain the greater involvement of females with kin in general, it neither explains why working class women tend to be less involved with their husband's kindred, nor does it clarify why working class males are "pulled" into associations with their wife's kindred to the neglect of their own. There is a two-fold problem here: First is the matter of the presumed pivotal role of the female in maintaining contact with both kindreds; second is the matter of visiting relatives jointly.

At the beginning of this chapter we suggested that each spouse plays a pivotal role in maintaining contacts with his or her own kindred. It would appear that this necessary condition is not being fulfilled by the husbands in these studies we have been reviewing. However, Young and Wilmott found that this was not exactly true, at least with respect to the husband's relationship with his parents. Although husbands had less contact with their own kindred than they had with their wife's kindred, Young and Wilmott (1957:73-74) found that the parents of these husbands are not neglected. They note that it was common for husbands to visit parents without the wife. In a sense this suggests that in their sample it is the husbands who maintain contact with both kindreds.

The question of whether married couples visit their respective kindred jointly (and what factors are associated with interaction with spouse's kindred) has not been thoroughly researched. Furthermore, there is some indication that joint visiting with relatives may be related to characteristics of the conjugal bond itself.

Many attempts have been made to analyze changing patterns in the conjugal relationship. Particular emphasis has been placed on the rise of companionship marriage, or what Young and Wilmott (1957:25) refer to as "the emerging partnership." This theoretical orientation attempts to relate community social structure to marital behavior. Using the conjugal relationship as the dependent variable, social structures providing continuity for social relationships—in particular kinship relations—are contrasted with social structures which do not provide for such continuity. The conjugal relationship is characterized as segregated in social structures which provide for continuity in external relationships, with each spouse working at tasks independently, and leisure time being spent apart from one another. In social structures that do not provide for the continuity of external social relationships, the conjugal relation is one in which it is likely that many activities and tasks are shared and leisure time is spent together (Mogey, 1964; Bott, 1957; and, Young and Wilmott, 1957).

The seminal work of Bott (1957) provides an excellent model for an examination of this matter. She suggests that a distinction should be made between joint conjugal role relationships and segregated conjugal role relationships. In the former, many activities within the household and without are pursued by the husband and wife together. With segregated conjugal role relationships, activities are carried out by the husband and wife, either without reference to one another or as part of a distinctive division of labor. Of particular interest is her suggestion (1957:60) that the degree of segregation in role relationships of husband and wife varies directly with the connectedness of the family's (i.e., domestic unit's) social network. By connectedness of the social network is meant the extent to which relatives and friends know and see one another. A network which is "loose knit" is one in which most of the people a person knows and contacts do not know or see one another, while a "closely knit social network" is one in which many of the people a person knows and sees do know and interact with one another. A close-knit social network can exert social control on its members; a loose-knit network cannot exert as much influence.

While the focus of Bott's study is not the problem we are examining (husband-wife differences in interaction with kindred), nevertheless her analysis is suggestive, particularly that aspect of it dealing with internal-external social relations of the conjugal unit. Since more highly segregated conjugal roles involve each spouse with different people outside the domestic unit, it would be less likely that these husbands and wives would visit relatives jointly or see their spouse's kindred. On the other hand, although husbands and wives who share activities might be more likely to visit relatives together, both might have less contact with kin because they concentrate on the conjugal relation itself. The wives in marriages with highly segregated conjugal roles would be more likely to have stronger ties with their own kindred than wives in marriages that involve more joint activities with their spouses. Additionally, we raise the question of the extent to which age differences between spouses can be used to interpret such internal-external interaction balances as these. For we know from the findings in the previous chapter that age is negatively associated with interaction with one's own close kindred and one's spouse's kindred.

In this chapter, then, we examine husband-wife differences in recruitment of kindred. At the heart of the issues we have discussed is the question of whether husbands and wives utilize differently the available opportunity structure of close and spouse's kindred. Do both husband and wife utilize the opportunity structure of the wife's kindred more fully than the husband's kindred? Are husbands pulled into the social orbit of their wives' kindred to the neglect of their own kindred? Do women play a pivotal role in maintaining contacts with both their own kindred and their spouse's kindred? Are the respective kindreds of each spouse seen jointly? And since we also wish to understand why differences between husbands and wives in contacting kindred might occur, we will also examine characteristics of the respondents and their marital relationships. Of particular concern, as we have mentioned, is the effect of the degree of conjugal role segregation on whether spouse's kindred are seen and whether kindred are seen jointly. And we will also examine how age and age differences between the conjugal partners are related to interaction patterns with kindred.

Husband-Wife Differences in Interaction

In this section we address ourselves to differences between husbands and wives in interaction with close and spouse's kindred. There are 530 married couples in the sample. Two different types of analysis will be followed. Some of the issues we have raised can be best examined by looking at differences between husbands and wives in recruitment of their respective close and spouse's kindred. Other questions are best examined by looking at differences among couples as a unit in interaction with kindred.

First we shall see whether there are differences between husbands and wives in recruitment of their respective close and spouse's kindred. These findings are presented in Tables 5-1 and 5-2. The first table presents data on whether the respondents saw any representative of these kindred at all. In addition, it arrays this information by geographical distance. Table 5-2 describes the utilization of the opportunity structures of close and spouse's kindred in terms of the number of available kindred seen and the frequency of interaction with kindred.[b]

Both tables indicate that large proportions of both husbands and wives see more representatives of the wife's close kindred more frequently than either of them sees the husband's close kindred. The totals presented in Table 5-1 clearly indicate that larger proportions of wives saw representatives of their close

---

[b]Number of available kindred seen and frequency of interaction with kindred, as above, are expressed by an index which has the property of controlling the number of representatives of a kindred available to respondents.

Table 5-1
Husbands and Wives Who Saw Available Close Kindred and
Spouse's Kindred, by Geographical Distance[a]
(In Percentages)

	Geographical Distance of Kindred	Close Kindred[b]	Spouse's Kindred[b]
Husbands[c]	Within six blocks	67.6 (71)	78.8 (85)
	Six blocks or more	47.2 (271)	56.4 (259)
Wives[c]	Within six blocks	79.8 (94)	71.4 (56)
	Six blocks or more	57.1 (312)	41.7 (218)
Total husbands[d]		54.2 (301)	65.2 (293)
Total wives[d]		64.5 (344)	49.4 (245)

[a]This table includes respondents who had either or both sets of relatives available to them.

[b]Percentages computed on the number of respondents reporting representatives of this kindred available to them in the metropolitan area.

[c]Fifty-one husbands and 56 wives did not report their respective spouse's kindred in the metropolitan area when their spouses did report their own close kindred available. Data presented in this chapter are based only on those respondents reporting kindred available.

[d]The (N)s appearing in the "Total" are not the sums of the cells in the body of the table because a number of respondents reported representatives of these kindred types in both geographical areas.

Table 5-2
Extent and Frequency of Contact with Close Kindred and
Spouse's Kindred Among Husbands and Wives

	Close Kindred			Spouse's Kindred		
	Mean Number Seen[a]	Mean Frequency of Contact[b]	(N)	Mean Number Seen	Mean Frequency of Contact	(N)
Husbands	.412	.642	(301)	.455	.936	(293)
Wives	.467	.967	(344)	.339	.626	(245)

[a]Range: 0-1

[b]Range: 0-7

kindred than husbands' kindred, and that larger proportions of husbands saw their wives' kindred than wives saw their husbands' kindred. In fact, a higher proportion of husbands (65.2 percent) saw representatives of their wives' kindred than saw representatives of their own close kindred (54.2 percent). However, the major difference lies in the much higher proportion of husbands who saw their spouses' kindred than wives who saw their husbands' kindred.

Moreover, we see in Table 5-1 that matrifocal residence is not an issue in this sample. For the numbers appearing in parenthesis in the body of the table show that a majority of husbands and wives do not report any representatives of their own kindred within six blocks of the home. And there is but a slight tendency for more women (N=94) than for men (N=71) to have close kindred within six blocks.

We also see in this table that geographical distance influences interaction with the kindred of both husband and wife equally. The proportion of husbands and wives who see relatives representing close kindred and spouse's kindred is markedly affected by whether they live within six blocks of, or six blocks or more, from their homes. Between 20 and 30 percent more husbands and wives see these kin if they are nearby. Within each geographical area we still find larger proportions of wives contacting their close kindred than husbands' kindred, and that larger proportions of husbands saw their wives' kindred than wives saw their husbands' kindred.

Table 5-2 shows that the available opportunity structure of close kindred and spouse's kindred is used differently by husbands and wives. While this holds for the number of kin seen, it is particularly evident in the frequency of contacts with kin. The mean contact scores indicate that spouse's kindred available to husbands were contacted about one and one-half times more frequently than their own available close kindred. But the opposite is true for wives.

Most studies of differences between husbands and wives in recruitment of their close and spouse's kindred do not carry the analysis beyond this point. And at the same time, most of these studies suggest that married males are pulled into association with their wives' kindred and that married women associate mainly with their own kindred. While the findings thus far presented apparently lend support to such a view, they are in fact insufficient, for we do not know the nature of the choices husbands and wives have for recruitment of kin or how such choices may influence the associations we have found and reported in Tables 5-1 and 5-2. That is, in order to examine the extent to which working class husbands see their wives' close kindred at the expense of seeing their own kindred, and to examine the extent to which working class wives fail to see their husbands' kindred while mainly interacting with their own close kindred, we must consider those respondents who had both choices available to them. That is, we must examine the choices of persons with both close and spouse's kindred residing in the metropolitan area. Husbands and wives who saw close and/or spouse's kindred (or who saw neither) among those who reported both types available to them are arrayed in Table 5-3.

Table 5-3
Husbands and Wives Who Saw Either Close Kindred, or Spouse's
Kindred, or Both, or Neither, When Both Were Available
(In Percentages)

	Respondents Who Saw Close and Spouse's Kindred	Respondents Who Saw Close Not Spouse's Kindred	Respondents Who Saw Spouse's But Not Close Kindred	Saw Neither	Total
Husbands	43.5	12.0	23.6	20.9	100 (191)
Wives	38.7	29.0	11.8	20.5	100 (186)

These findings raise questions regarding the conventional interpretation of matricentricity: that husbands are "pulled" into the social arena of the inlaws to the neglect of their own kindred. The modal pattern for husbands as well as wives is to see both types of kindred. However, if there is selectivity in interaction with relatives, it is clearly the wife's kindred that will be seen. More wives saw *only* their close kindred (29.0 percent) and fewer saw *only* their spouse's kindred (11.8 percent). Just the opposite is true for the husbands: 12 percent saw *only* their close kindred while about 24 percent saw *only* their wives' kindred.

Although this evidence might be taken to support the view that husbands are pulled into interaction with their inlaws, a slightly higher proportion of husbands (43.5 percent) than wives (38.7 percent) saw both types of kindred. Thus while wives tend more to see only their close kindred than only spouse's kindred, and husbands to see only their spouse's kindred than their own close kindred, a larger proportion of husbands than wives see both types of kindred. Altogether, these findings imply that it is at least (if not more) correct to say women are not pulled into interaction with their inlaws, as to say that husbands are pulled into interaction with theirs.

Since husbands more than wives maintain a balance in contact with both kindreds when both were available, these findings question whether husbands see their inlaws at the expense of seeing their own kindred. However, the greater female involvement with their own close kindred remains. Since women are more active in the performance of kinship duties than men, one would expect to find—as we have—that more wives see their close kindred than husbands see *their* close kindred. Perhaps the entrenchment of these women in obligations with their own kindred explains why these wives do not see their husband's kindred. We shall have more to say about this presumed imbalance between the sexes later in this chapter.

The disproportionate number of husbands who saw only their spouse's kindred may not be a consequence of being "pulled" from their own kindred, but an indication that they visit relatives with their wives whose primary obligations lie with representatives of their own close kindred. On the other hand these working class wives may fail to see their husbands' kindred because they find it difficult to extricate themselves from obligations to their own kindred.

If working class women do not see their husbands' kindred because of obligations to their own kindred, then one would expect to find that a higher proportion of wives whose close kindred are not living in the area would be more likely to see their husband's kindred than women for whom both close and spouse's kindred are available. But we see in Table 5-3 that of the 186 wives who reported both types of kindred available, a total of 50.5 percent (those who saw both kindreds plus those who saw only spouse's kindred) saw their husbands' kindred. This percentage is similar to—but slightly higher than—the percentage of wives who saw their husbands' kindred (45 percent—not shown in the table) when representatives of their own kindred were *not* available. Thus the thesis that obligations to their own kindred prevent working class women from seeing their husbands' kindred is not supportable.

So far, then, we lack a clear basis for understanding why more married women do not see their spouses' kindred. It does not appear to be due to obligations to their own kindred. And as far as husbands are concerned, although a higher proportion of them saw their spouses' kindred than their own close kindred, the data do not indicate that they saw their spouses' kindred at the expense of seeing their own close kindred. This is clearly demonstrated by the additional fact that there is little difference in the proportion of husbands who saw their close kindred when their spouses' kindred were available (55.5 percent in Table 5-3—those who saw both plus those who saw only close kindred) and when their spouses' kindred were not available (51.3 percent—not shown in the table).

To understand differences between husbands and wives in interaction with their respective spouses' kindred, we must put the question a little differently and turn to a slightly different type of analysis. We must determine whether both husband and wife each play pivotal roles in contacting their respective close kindred or whether this responsibility falls primarily upon the wives. If both husband and wife play pivotal roles in contacting their respective close kindred, when kindred are not seen jointly by the conjugal pair, both husband and wife will be more likely to see their *own* close kindred separately than either will be to see their spouse's kindred separately. If this responsibility falls primarily upon the wife, then, when the conjugal pair do not see kindred jointly, the kindred will be seen by the wife.

In Tables 5-4 and 5-5, the conjugal pair is examined as a unit. The tables show whether close kindred of the husband and the wife are seen jointly by the conjugal pair (and, if they are not, what the nature is of this imbalance). Table

Table 5-4
Married Couples Who Saw Kindred Jointly and Separately[a]
(In Percentages)

	Husband's Close Kindred	Wife's Close Kindred
Both husband and wife saw kindred	45.3	61.4
Only husband saw kindred	9.4	3.8
Only wife saw kindred	4.1	5.5
Neither saw kindred	41.2	29.4
Total	100.0 (245)	100.0 (293)

[a]Based on couples who agree that the relatives in question live in the metropolitan area.

Table 5-5
Of Married Couples Who Saw Kindred Jointly, Those Who
Also Saw Equal and Unequal Numbers of Kindred[a]
(In Percentages)

	Husband's Close Kindred	Wife's Close Kindred
Both husband and wife saw the same number of kindred	74.8	76.1
Husband saw more kindred than wife	17.1	6.1
Wife saw more kindred than husband	8.1	17.7
Total	100.0 (111)	100.0 (180)

[a]Based on couples who agree that the relatives in question live in the metropolitan area.

5-4 shows the proportion of married couples who had any contact with close kindred jointly and those husbands and wives who saw kindred separately. It reveals that for the majority of these couples, the close kindred of each spouse are seen either by both husband and wife or not at all. Since a high proportion of these couples either saw close kindred of each spouse jointly or not at all, the evidence to support or refute the view that both husband and wife play the pivotal role in contacting their own respective kindred rests on a small foundation. But what evidence exists does show that when kindred are seen separately the husband as well as the wife are more likely to see their own close kindred (separately) than to see their spouse's kindred (separately). Consistent with the previous findings is the fact that it is more likely that the husband's close kindred (41.5 percent) than the wife's close kindred (29.4 percent) are *not* seen at all, and more likely that the wife's close kindred (61.4 percent) than the husband's close kindred (45.3 percent) will be the recipient of a joint visit.

Table 5-5 extracts those couples in Table 5-4 who contacted kindred jointly and shows the proportion who saw equal numbers of each kindred jointly, as well as the proportion of husbands and wives who in addition to joint contact saw unequal numbers of these kindred; that is, who saw some of these relatives separately. These data support the view that each spouse plays a pivotal role in contacting his or her own close kindred. When these couples do not see exactly the same number of a kindred jointly, both husband and wife are likely to see more of their own close kindred than their spouse's kindred. But most of those who see kindred jointly do not also contact these kindred separately from their spouse. For, as Table 5-5 shows, approximately 75 percent of the couples who contacted kindred jointly saw exactly the same number of husband's and wife's kindred.

In the light of this joint visiting pattern, we may clearly suggest that the reason wives fail to see their husband's close kindred is because husbands are not seeing them. And husbands see their wives' close kindred because their wives see their own close kindred.

The essential correctness of this analysis may be seen in the cases where the consanguinal-affinal distinction by definition do not exist—namely, in the recruitment of joint descendant kindred for interaction. Here we would expect to find only symmetry in the interaction patterns of husband and wife with their adult children. Furthermore, we would expect no differences by sex of joint descendant kin in their interaction with either of their parents, the husband or wife of reference. In addition, since crossing the affinal line is not at issue, there is little reason to expect any parent-child contact to occur in the absence of one or the other parents—the husbands and wives of our sample.

In Table 5-6 we array the joint and the separate interaction of husband and wife with their sons and daughters. Our expectations are fully borne out. Almost no interaction takes place between children with one parent alone, regardless of the sex of either parent or child. And among the minute numbers of one-parent interactions there is no pattern related to sex of parent and child. What is abundantly clear from these data is the joint interaction pattern: that is, either children are seen by both parents together or they are not seen at all by their parents.

Thus, the pattern of interaction observed in the lateral extension among close and spouse's kindred descends across the generation line in terms of joint visiting. However, we also see that neither husband nor wife plays a pivotal role

Table 5-6

Married Couples Who Saw Joint Descendant Kindred Jointly and Separately (In Percentages)

	Son	Daughter
Both husband and wife saw	(118) 80.3	(160) 88.4
Only husband saw	(4) 2.7	(4) 2.2
Only wife saw	(3) 2.0	(3) 1.7
Neither saw	(22) 15.0	(14) 7.7
Total	(147) 100.0	(181) 100.0

in contacting children who are by their nature kindred of both. We do not find in Table 5-6 what we found in Tables 5-4 and 5-3, where each spouse plays a pivotal role in contacting his or her own kindred. For, which adult children are not seen jointly, both husband and wife are equally likely to contact them separately.

It is our contention that the difference between contacts with one's own kindred and contacts with spouse's kindred lies in the fact that one's spouse becomes an important intermediary link in contacting spouse's kindred, whereas no such link is necessary in recruitment of one's own kindred, whether they are joint descendants, close kindred, or distant kindred.

Returning to the issue of matricentricity, then, several conclusions can be drawn from the findings presented thus far: (1) more wives see their close kindred than husbands see their own close kindred; (2) more husbands see their wives' kindred than wives see their husbands' kindred; (3) the presence or absence of the wife's kindred in the pool of relatives is neither related to fewer husbands seeing their close kindred nor to fewer wives seeing their husbands' kindred; (4) both husband and wife play a pivotal role in contacting their own kindred; and (5) the first and second of these conclusions are related since representatives of these kindred are seen jointly by the conjugal pair in most instances.

The working class conjugal family, then, exists in a system of kindred-based linkages tending toward a balance such that each spouse plays a pivotal role in contacting his or her own close kindred. It is reinforced by the ideal norms of our society that a married person is expected to treat his own and his spouse's kin equally for interaction (Komarovsky, 1962:244-245). Consequently, each spouse in principle ought to achieve parity of contact between his or her own and partner's close consanguines. When this does not occur it may be due to other factors related to the system of kinship—although perhaps not necessarily constituent of it. Therefore, our next task is to gain a better understanding of why more wives see their close kindred than husbands see *their* close kindred. Since the close kindred of the husband and of the wife are for the most part seen jointly, we will also be able to understand why the husbands are more involved with their wives kindred. Or, to put it another way, why are wives' linkages to close kindred operated to a greater degree than husbands'.

Husband-Wife Age Differences
and Interaction

It is common knowledge that women in our society tend to marry men somewhat older than themselves. The age composition of the conjugal pairs in the sector of the working class we have sampled exemplifies this difference between ages of spouses. The modal age grouping of married men (41.1 percent) in the sample is 65 and over. But the modal age of married women (41.3 percent) is 54 and under. In all the marriages in which the husband is age 65 or more, fully 46 percent of the wives are age 64 or less; and in all the marriages in which the husband is between ages 55 and 64, 45 percent of the wives are age 54 or less.

We have seen in the preceding chapter that the age of the respondents is negatively associated with recruitment of close kindred for interaction. The disproportionate representation of husbands in older age categories raises the question of whether the differences in recruitment of close kindred between husbands and wives might be a function of the fact that husbands tend to be older than their wives.

Table 5-7 indicates that when age is held constant, the differences between husbands and wives in the number of those who saw any of their available close kindred is considerably reduced, from what was reported in Table 5-1, among two of the three age groupings we are considering here. That is, among working class people age 55 to 64, only 5 percent more wives than husbands saw close kindred, a rather negligible difference in any case. And among those over age 65 not only is predominance of the wife's contact with close kin erased, but 5 percent more *husbands* than wives see any of these relatives. Thus the substantially higher proportion of wives than husbands seeing their close kindred is a phenomenon limited to those working class people in the younger age range of our sample only—that is, between 45 and 54 years of age.

Do differences between husbands and wives in the extent and frequency with which they utilize the opportunity structure of close kindred diminish when age is held constant? Indices representing the mean number of contacts and the mean number of close kindred seen by husbands and wives at different age levels are presented in Table 5-8.

Differences between the mean number of close kindred seen by husbands and

Table 5-7

Husbands and Wives Who Saw Available Close Kindred and Spouse's Kindred, by Age (In Percentages)

Age		Close Kindred	Spouse's Kindred	Spouse's Kindred By Age of Spouse
65 and over	Husbands	42.3 (104)	56.1 (107)	47.5 (61)
	Wives	38.0 (71)	31.8 (44)	41.4 (70)
55-64	Husbands	53.5 (86)	59.0 (83)	58.0 (88)
	Wives	58.9 (107)	45.2 (73)	41.4 (70)
54 and under	Husbands	65.8 (111)	79.6 (103)	77.1 (144)
	Wives	79.5 (166)	57.8 (128)	64.0 (89)
Gamma:	Husbands	−.320	−.348	−.429
	Wives	−.544	−.332	−.317

wives at each age level reflect the pattern of contact with close kindred revealed in Table 5-7. That is, when age is controlled, wives do not necessarily exceed husbands in terms of the number of close kindred seen. For, among people age 65 and over, as well as those between ages 55 to 64, husbands see larger mean numbers of close kindred than wives. It is only among the youngest age grouping in our sample, those who are 54 and under, that wives still surpass husbands in this respect.

However, Table 5-8 also shows that in terms of the frequency with which close kindred are seen wives still exceed husbands at every age level. The significance of age, then, is that it restricts the number of kin seen by wives and husbands both; but this restriction is stronger for wives, so that husbands end up interacting with larger numbers of close kindred. But wives apparently make up for this by maintaining a higher mean frequency of contact than husbands, albeit with fewer relatives. The wives compensate for diminished scope by increasing the intensity of interaction. (It should be noted, though, that these differences between husbands and wives in frequency of contact, with age held constant, are nevertheless smaller than the differences we found before holding age constant.)

We must now relate the findings that (1) the opportunity structure of spouse's kindred is differentially utilized by husbands and wives; and (2) married couples see their kindred jointly.

Table 5-8
Extent and Frequency of Contact with Close and Spouse's Kindred Among Husbands and Wives, by Age

Age		Close Kindred			Spouse's Kindred			Spouse's Kindred By Age of Spouse		
		Mean Number Seen	Mean Frequency of Contact	(N)	Mean Number Seen	Mean Frequency of Contact	(N)	Mean Number Seen	Mean Frequency of Contact	(N)
65 and over	Husbands	.315	.471	(104)	.404	.768	(107)	.334	.774	(61)
	Wives	.266	.553	(71)	.264	.553	(44)	.325	.552	(86)
55-64	Husbands	.510	.553	(86)	.395	.801	(83)	.419	.870	(88)
	Wives	.435	.891	(107)	.350	.501	(73)	.247	.430	(70)
54 and under	Husbands	.428	.870	(111)	.556	1.219	(103)	.534	1.015	(144)
	Wives	.573	1.087	(166)	.358	.723	(128)	.424	.888	(89)

Age difference between the conjugal pairs is a major reason why husbands are more involved with their wives' kindred than their own. A partial explanation for wives not seeing as much of their husbands' kindred, and husbands seeing more of their wives' kindred, lies in the fact that men are generally older than their wives. Since age of married respondents is clearly linked with recruitment of close kindred, and since most respondents see close kindred with their husband or wife, the variable that is meaningfully related to the recruitment of spouse's kindred is not the age of the respondent, but rather his or her spouse's age.

Data pertaining to patterns of recruitment of spouse's kindred among husbands and wives are also presented in Tables 5-7 and 5-8. In the second column of these tables, the data are arrayed by age of respondents. In the third column of Tables 5-7 and 5-8 the data are arrayed by age of the respondent's spouse.

Examination of patterns of interaction with spouse's kindred by age of respondent (column two) indicates that at each age level more husbands than wives see their spouse's kindred (Table 5-7); and that the opportunity structure of spouse's kindred (Table 5-8) is more fully utilized by husbands—particularly in terms of frequency of contact—than by wives. This is quite complementary to the pattern of interaction with close kindred and is precisely what is expected if joint visiting by the spouses is the norm.

However, examining patterns of interaction with spouse's kindred by age of respondent's spouse (third column) suggests again that the differences between husband and wife are partly understandable as a function of the age differences which we have just elucidated. That is, when the age of the spouse rather than the age of the respondent, is held constant, the differences between husbands and wives in contacts with spouse's kindred are reduced for the most part. This pattern of reduced differences between husbands and wives in contact with spouse's kindred holds for respondents whose spouse's were age 65 and over and for those whose spouses were age 54 and under. It does not hold for respondents whose spouses were between the ages of 55 and 64.

Despite the fact that differences between husbands and wives are reduced by holding the respondents' spouses' age constant rather than holding the respondents' ages constant, some of the differences by sex do remain. Regardless of the respondents' spouses' ages, the opportunity structure of spouses' kindred is more fully utilized by husbands than by wives, both in terms of extensity and frequency of interaction (Table 5-8).

When we examine the wives' recruitment of their husbands' kindred by the ages of their husbands, we find that the figures are roughly comparable to their husbands' recruitment of their own close kindred. The husbands' recruitment of their wives' kindred is also similar to the wives' recruitment of their own close kindred.[c] This suggests that the differences between husbands and wives in recruitment of their spouses' kindred is understandable as a consequence of the pivotal role the husbands and wives play in maintaining contacts with their own kindred.

Thus, one reason husbands do not see their own close kindred is that they are generally older than their wives. And being generally younger than their husbands, wives are also more active in seeing their own close kindred. Inasmuch as close kindred are seen jointly, age differences between husbands and wives also provide a rationale for the observation that more husbands than wives are involved in interaction with their spouse's kindred. Husbands with younger wives see their wives' close kindred because these younger women are more likely to see their close kindred.

But still residual differences remain, as we have said. And these are no doubt due to other factors. We turn now to explore one which is likely to throw additional light on the matricentricity issue.

Conjugal Role Segregation and Husband-Wife Differences in Interaction

In the preceding section we found that differences in contact with kindred are related both to age of and age differences between husbands and wives. Now we will examine whether a crucial characteristic of the conjugal bond itself has any bearing on the patterns of interaction we have found among husbands and wives in their contact with kindred. The choice of this characteristic of the conjugal bond, namely conjugal role segregation, is dictated by the dynamic of husband-wife interaction with their own and each others' kindred.

For once it is realized that the conjugal pair is a dyad in which each partner serves as the pivotal individual for the other in relationships with respective close kindred certain questions naturally arise. They concern, of course, the idea that a balance in the initiation and conduct of kinship interaction may well be associated with other balances or symmetries within the conjugal unit; and the presence or absence of such balances or symmetries could play a role in maintaining a matricentric, patricentric, or equalitarian pattern of kinship interaction.

What, then, is the relation between the degree of conjugal role segregation

---

[c]As previously noted, some husbands and wives did not report their spouses' kindred in metropolitan Philadelphia when their spouses reported close kindred available. The figures in Table 6-7 comparing recruitment of spouses' kindred by age of spouse and recruitment of close kindred by age of respondents would probably be more comparable were it not for this discrepancy in reporting.

and the extent to which kindred are seen jointly? Are married couples with highly segregated conjugal roles less likely to see close kindred jointly than couples with a low degree of conjugal role segregation? What is the association between degree of conjugal role segregation and contact with spouse's kindred?

A conjugal role segregation index was created from responses to nine questions on the interview schedule. The questions elicited information about who made decisions in the household and who carried out certain domestic tasks. They concerned activities such as grocery shopping and keeping track of money and bills, and domestic decisions such as buying insurance, budgeting, choice of living quarters, and so on.[d] Each activity or decision in which the husband and wife shared equally was assigned a value of one and a score of zero was given for each activity or decision made separately or not at all. Hence, scores range from zero to nine. Four our purposes, marriage is characterized as having highly segregated conjugal roles when the score is between zero and four. A marriage is defined as having a low degree of conjugal role segregation when the respondents' score is between five and nine.[e]

The first question we address is whether there are differences in contact with spouse's kindred by degree of conjugal role segregation. As we have noted, the issue is rather complex. Here we may phrase it as a question of whether a marriage that does not involve the husband and wife in cooperative domestic activities (that is, one that is role segregated) limits the partners' relationships with their respective spouse's kindred. We are suggesting that a distinctive division of labor and lack of joint activities within the household (that is, highly segregated conjugal roles) is likely to be associated with failure to see spouse's kindred. While, on the other hand, joint participation in household activities and decision making may be associated with other joint activities including seeing

---

[d]The questions were worded as follows: "We would like to know how you and your (husband) (wife) divide up some of the family jobs. Who does the grocery shopping, for example? Who does the evening dishes? Who repairs things around the house? Who keeps track of the money and the bills?" A second question was asked: "In every family somebody has to decide such things as where the family will live and so on. Many couples talk such things over first, but the *final* decision often has to be made by the husband or the wife. For instance, who usually makes the final decision about whether or not to buy some life insurance? What house or apartment to take? How much money your family can afford to spend per week on food? Whether to see a doctor when someone isn't feeling well? About what to do on a Sunday afternoon?" The responses to these items were then coded according to whether usually the husband, the wife, both equally, or neither performs these tasks and makes these decisions.

[e]Among the 530 married couples, there was 84 percent agreement in the scores representing the degree of conjugal role segregation. That is, when the wife's responses to the questions on the interview schedule were matched with their husband's responses, 84 percent of the 530 couples agreed on the number of activities and tasks shared jointly and separately. According to the wives' responses, 60 percent of the couples had highly segregated conjugal roles. The corresponding figure by the husbands' responses is 57 percent. In the following analysis we will use only the wives' responses to the questions we have been discussing as a measure of the degree of segregation of conjugal roles. No systematic bias is introduced by using the wife's score rather than the husband's.

spouse's kindred. The relation between seeing spouse's kindred and the degree of conjugal role segregation, holding age of respondent constant, is shown in Table 5-9 for husbands and wives.

The column totals in Table 5-9 show that the degree of conjugal role segregation is negatively related to seeing spouse's kindred for both husband and wife. That is, highly segregated conjugal roles limit contact with spouse's kindred, while a low degree of conjugal role segregation is associated with larger proportions of husbands and wives seeing spouse's kindred. Since this association affects the husbands' as well as the wives' contacts with their inlaws, our previous findings have not been altered. Regardless of the degree of conjugal role segregation, a higher proportion of husbands than wives saw their spouse's kindred. In addition, this negative association between conjugal role segregation and contact with spouse's kindred remains, for both husband and wife, when age of respondents is held constant. However, there is a rough difference in the degree of this association at different age levels. The association between conjugal role segregation and contact with spouse's kindred is stronger among husbands and wives 55 years old and over than it is for husbands and wives 54 and under.

Thus far we have found that the degree of conjugal role segregation is inversely related to seeing spouse's kindred. The remaining task is to determine

Table 5-9

Husbands and Wives Who Saw Spouse's Kindred, by Conjugal Role Segregation Score, and by Age (In Percentages)

Age		High Conjugal Role Segregation	Low Conjugal Role Segregation
65 and over	Husbands	49.2 (59)	64.6 (48)
	Wives	26.9 (26)	38.9 (18)
55-64	Husbands	50.9 (55)	75.0 (28)
	Wives	39.1 (46)	55.6 (27)
54 and under	Husbands	80.6 (62)	78.0 (41)
	Wives	53.7 (82)	65.2 (46)
Totals	Husbands	60.8 (176)	71.8 (117)
	Wives	44.8 (154)	57.1 (91)

whether conjugal role segregation is also related to seeing kindred jointly. Data on this question are presented in Tables 5-10 and 5-11.

Table 5-10
Married Couples Who Saw Close Kindred Jointly and Separately, by Conjugal Role Segregation Score (In Percentages)

	Husband's Close Kindred		Wife's Close Kindred	
	Conjugal Role Segregation			
	High	Low	High	Low
Both husband and wife saw kindred	42.8	49.4	57.9	66.7
Only husband saw kindred	11.0	6.6	2.8	5.2
Only wife saw kindred	2.0	7.7	6.3	4.3
Neither saw kindred	44.2	36.3	32.9	23.9
Total	100.0 (154)	100.0 (91)	100.0 (176)	100.0 (117)

Table 5-11
Of Married Couples Who Saw Kindred Jointly, Those Who Also Saw Equal and Unequal Numbers of Kindred, by Conjugal Role Segregation Score (In Percentages)

	Husband's Close Kindred		Wife's Close Kindred	
	Conjugal Role Segregation			
	High	Low	High	Low
Both husband and wife saw the same number of kindred	72.7	77.8	74.5	78.2
Husband saw more representatives of kindred	19.7	13.3	3.9	9.0
Wife saw more representatives of kindred	7.6	8.9	21.6	12.8
Total	100.0 (66)	100.0 (45)	100.0 (102)	100.0 (78)

Table 5-10 shows the proportion of married couples who had any contact with their close kindred jointly, and those husbands and wives who saw close kindred separately, by high and low conjugal role segregation. A somewhat higher proportion of couples who scored low on the conjugal role segregation index saw kindred jointly than couples who had highly segregated conjugal roles. This holds for joint visiting with the husband's close kindred and for joint visiting with the wife's close kindred. Furthermore, there are differences by degree of conjugal role segregation in contacting kindred separately. When kindred were not seen jointly, husbands and wives who scored low on the index were about equally as likely to see their own kindred as their spouse's kindred separately. And also, as we would expect, husbands and wives who had highly segregated conjugal roles were more likely to see their own kindred separately than their spouse's kindred separately.

Table 5-11 extracts from Table 5-10 those couples who contacted kindred jointly and shows the proportion who saw equal numbers of representatives of close kindred jointly and those husbands and wives who saw unequal numbers of such kindred by high or low conjugal role segregation. Table 5-11 shows that conjugal role segregation is also associated with seeing equal numbers of kindred jointly. A slightly smaller proportion of couples who had high conjugal role segregation scores contacted the same number of representatives of the husband's kindred and equal numbers of the wife's kindred than couples who had low scores. In addition, both husbands and wives with high conjugal role segregation saw more representatives of their own close kindred separately than those who had low role segregation scores. But these differences are quite small.

Thus we see that when couples share in decision making and other activities within the household, each partner is more likely to see his or her spouse's kindred, and they are more likely to visit kindred jointly. Highly segregated conjugal roles, on the other hand, seem to be reflected in reduced joint visiting, seeing less of spouse's kindred, and increased contact with one's own kindred without the presence of one's spouse.

In sum, the evidence presented in this section reveals that the symmetry of the dyadic balance through which conjugal partners initiate and maintain interaction with their respective close and spouse's kindred has a counterpart in the division of labor and decision making within the conjugal unit. We do not want to prejudge the question of precedence—whether the balanced linkage interaction pattern produces the internal sharing of tasks and decisions, or whether the joint participation in tasks and decision making within the conjugal unit lead to the kinship interaction pattern that seems to typify this working class population. This is not an issue which can be resolved with the data available here. For present purposes, though, it is sufficient to establish the internal-external dynamic of conjugal pair interaction, within itself and with kindred.

Conclusion

In this chapter we have examined husband-wife differences in interaction patterns with kindred. Our initial findings indicated that wives are more involved in interaction with their close kindred than either they or their husbands are involved in interaction with the husbands' close kindred.

We have attempted to provide an understanding of why husbands are more likely to see their wives' kindred than their own kindred, and why wives do not see their husbands' kindred but do see their own close kindred. And we have found that husbands are included by their wives in joint visiting of her close kindred. However, husbands do not necessarily see their wives' kindred at the expense of seeing their own kindred. The entrenchment of wives in activities with their own kindred has not been found to be associated with the fact that they and their husbands do not see his kindred.

In no way do our findings support Adams's and Robins and Tomanec's view that women act as representatives of the domestic unit in contacting relatives, that they play a pivotal role in interaction with relatives. To the contrary, we are led to conclude that both husband and wife play a pivotal role in providing linkages to interaction with their respective close kindred in the working class. If the husband does not see his close kindred, the wife will not see his kindred; if the wife does not see her close kindred, the husband will not see her kindred. When representatives of a kindred are seen, they are either seen by both the husband and the wife or by the spouse for whom these relatives are close kindred.

Moreover, what has been regarded as a matricentric bias in kinship interaction in the working class has a different meaning from what was previously thought. It is not that the wife fails to fulfill her obligations to contact her husband's kin, but rather that the husband fails to provide this necessary link with his close consanguines. In the cases in which the husband does provide this link, wives also contact them. Likewise, husbands are not pulled into interaction with their wives' kindred to the neglect of their own, but rather accompany their wives when their wives see their own kindred.

One reason these working class wives do not see their husbands' kindred is that their husbands are not seeing them. Husbands, on the other hand, are seeing their wives' close kindred because their wives see them.

The greater involvement of the wives in interaction with their own close kindred than either husbands' or wives' involvement with the husband's close kindred is associated with age differences between husbands and wives. Holding age of respondents constant reduces the differences between husbands and wives in contacts with their respective close kindred—thus another reason husbands do not see their own close kindred is that they are generally older than their wives.

Age differences also provide a partial rationale for why the wives are more active in seeing their own close kindred: most wives are younger than their husbands. Since kindred are seen jointly, age differences between husbands and wives also provide a partial explanation of why more husbands than wives are involved in interaction with their spouse's kindred. Husbands with younger wives see their wives' close kindred because these younger women are more likely to see their own close kindred. To a considerable extent, then, so-called matricentric bias is not a function of kinship (hence the term matricentric is misleading), but rather is an artifact of the age differences in the conjugal pair.

We also examined whether the role relationship between husband and wife was associated with seeing kindred jointly and with recruitment of spouse's kindred. The issue here concerned the question of how characteristics of the internal dynamics of a marriage are associated with social relationships with available kindred outside the household of the marital pair. A measure of the way various decisions and household activities and tasks were organized by these couples was used as an index of conjugal role segregation. Although our problem focus is quite different from Bott's, our findings lend support to her general assumption that there is a relationship between the internal role relationship within a marriage and the partners' external social relationships. That is, the degree of conjugal role segregation is associated with variation in seeing spouse's kindred and seeing kindred jointly.

Married couples who did not share in household tasks and activities (i.e., those with highly segregated conjugal roles) were less likely than those who did share in these activities (low conjugal role segregation) to see kindred jointly and to see spouse's kindred. Highly segregated conjugal role relationships would seem to place constraints on seeing spouse's kindred and seeing kindred jointly, while low conjugal role segregation facilitates joint visiting and seeing spouse's kindred for both husband and wife. The more a couple share domestic activities together, the more likely it is that they will also participate as a couple in their external relationshps.

The degree of role segregation between husband and wife functions somewhat like age: it is a factor which in itself has little to do with kinship qua kinship. But taking account of conjugal role segregation also reduces the level of matricentricity reflected in interaction with kin. The influence of age and conjugal role segregation, and doubtless also other factors we have been unable to examine here, provide evidence for the notion that the kindred-based linkage system of kinship interaction is essentially balanced across the marital relation. Moreover, this is a culturally sanctioned balance which, when it is altered matricentrically or patricentrically, is altered by factors like age and conjugal role segregation, which are in themselves extraneous to kinship. We contend that the normative prescript of equalitarian treatment of the kindred of each spouse in social relations is the prime kinship obligation bearing upon husband-wife variability in interaction with their own and each others relatives.

That departures from culturally prescribed patterns of behavior occur is, of course, well known. In this case they are due to factors such as the availability of categories of relatives, discrepancy in age between spouses, the degree of conjugal role segregation within the marriage, and no doubt other conditions as well. And it is these that gross measures of husband-wife differences in interaction often reflect. However, as we have made clear in this chapter, to term these differences functions of kinship is an error. In the working class, at least, the ideal is equality of husband and wife in interaction with respective close kindred. Conjugal variability in kinship interaction is produced by nonkinship departures from the ideal.

6

Kindred-Based Linkages: A Model of Working Class Kinship Interaction

We have been pointing out in the preceding chapters that current approaches and conceptualizations do not permit a systematic description and analysis of the kinship system of the United States in structural-relational terms. We have noted where they fail to account for the complexities involved in the highly differentiated relational kinship structure existing among urban, working class people such as those who comprise our sample. We have suggested a kindred-based linkage model as an alternative to existing conceptions. Without this model of kinship relationships, some of the underlying bases of differential recruitment we have reported would not have been seen.

In addition, at various points in the analysis of data on interaction presented thus far, we have suggested that the normative aspect of kinship has been neglected and that kinship norms cannot be understood, moreover, in terms of sentiments developed in the nuclear family. Thus the question, What is the nature of the morality governing extra-familial kin ties? has not been raised by most sociological researchers working in this area.

We intend to begin to provide an answer to this question and simultaneously to further develop our model of kindred-based linkages. To accomplish these goals we must determine more clearly how the normative system operates in kinship interaction. Of primary importance are the interrelated questions of: the bases on which choices in recruitment of kin are made; the relative social significance of consanguinal ties as opposed to relations with affines; and the consequent balances or imbalances that occur across the consanguinal-affinal axis.

Consanguines and Affines

Choices in recruitment of kin on the part of our working class respondents must be considered in light of the sanctions that can be brought to bear on an individual by his kin. This view is particularly helpful in contrasting relations with affines and consanguines, for the sanctions that may be brought to bear in recruitment of representatives of one's own consanguinal kindred may differ from those involved in recruitment of affines. This suggests a differential basis for choice in recruitment of these two distinct types of relatives—which difference was evident in the preceding chapter. In fact, to speak of ego's choice in contacts with his spouse's kindred seems somewhat misleading since spouse's kin are not seen by respondents unless the spouse also sees them.

113

The related question of the social significance of consanguinal kindred ties and those with affines is critical. We are not certain whether different kinship norms attach to consanguinal kindred relations as opposed to relations with affines, or whether the same norms of kinship apply equally to both. As is suggested by the differential basis for choice in recruitment, and also by data from previous chapters, there is some support for the view that different kinship norms may be in operation across the consanguinal-affinal axis, at least with respect to close and spouse's kindred. We have found that these affines and consanguines were not equally important in interaction terms to respondents. Not only is contact with spouse's kindred dependent on the continued existence of the marital bond, suggesting different kinship norms, but when the bond is intact, it also depends on ego's spouse in providing the necessary link.

In view of findings such as these, it is necessary to examine differences in recruitment of consanguines and affines more closely. Ego's recruitment of all affinal kin—those married to his own consanguines as well as affines by his own marriage—may take place in the absence of sanctions which might be imposed were they consanguines. Moreover, ego's recruitment of all affinal kin may be contingent on intermediary relatives (such as his spouse, his siblings, and his adult children) rather than on himself alone. This would make interaction with affines less important inasmuch as it would not be established or maintained independently from other kin. Thus focal ego's interaction with the general category of affines may be contingent on connecting relatives. If this turned out to be so, we would have more certain evidence that the same norms of kinship do not apply to both consanguines and affines, and we would know better the sense in which one can speak of a normative aspect of affinal kin relations.

But despite the fact that kinship norms may differ between consanguines and affines, social relations with affines may be more significant in our society than in other societies, given the emphasis on the conjugal bond as a solidary one. Thus we raise the question of the extent to which relations with kindred and affines are balanced. From the point of view of kinship interaction, this question bears on the extent to which there is symmetry in recruitment along the consanguinal-affinal axis of married couples and balance across the marital axis of the husband's kindred and the wife's kindred.

Since the kinship system places a structural premium on both husband and wife in the maintenance of continuity of relationships with their own kindred, it follows that the pivotal role spouses play may well exemplify a major feature of the entire relational system. The extent to which contacts with affines can occur may not only depend on the extent to which ego promotes these relationships—which is where Schneider, Parsons, and others seem to leave us—but also on the extent to which ego's intermediary kin (his kindred and those of his spouse) do this as well.

In view of the foregoing discussion and the problems raised, a more literal analysis of the role structure of an individual's universe of kin is required, one involving separate treatment of categories of relatives we have treated as types of kindred. We are concerned here with the extent to which there is differential treatment in terms of interaction of all categories of affines and consanguines; and we seek to determine whether ego's consanguines and his spouse's consanguines serve as connecting links to all these affines. Since our focus is on the consanguinal-affinal dimension, we will separate ego's siblings and siblings' spouses from the general category of close kindred. For the same reasons we will separate ego's adult children and his adult children's spouses from the general category of joint descendants. To lend additional insight into the affinal dimension of kinship, we will also separate ego's spouse's siblings and his spouse's siblings' spouses from the general category of spouse's kindred.

These distinctions create two categories of consanguinal kin: collaterally we have ego's siblings, and intergenerationally we have his adult children. Along the affinal axis there are four categories: collaterally we have ego's siblings' spouses, ego's spouse's siblings, and ego's spouse's siblings' spouses; intergenerationally we have ego's adult children's spouses.

In making these added distinctions we can examine how respondents recruit kin along the consanguinal-affinal axis and in this way shed more light on the question of the significance of relationships with consanguines as opposed to those with affines. We can also examine the related question of the extent to which relationships with affines are symmetrical but at the same time contingent on ego's relationships with connecting kin. For to understand differences in recruitment of consanguines and affines who are married pairs, we must determine whether respondents contact them jointly as a couple or whether they are seen separately; and among those seen separately, whether there is differential treatment along the consanguinal-affinal axis. Moreover, we wish to see whether there are differences in recruitment of ego's own consanguines and their spouses and his recruitment of his spouse's consanguines and their spouses.

If consanguinal kin are more important to respondents than affines, then respondents will be more likely to see consanguines separately from consanguines' spouses. If there is no differential treatment along this axis, then consanguines and affines will be equally likely to be seen as reflected in contacting them jointly as a couple and in seeing them equally when seen separately. And if there is no difference in recruitment of ego's consanguines and their spouses (close kindred) and his recruitment of spouse's consanguines and their spouses (spouse's kindred), the same pattern—differential treatment or lack of same—would obtain with both. That is, a balanced system across the husband-wife relation requires ego to treat his spouse's consanguines and his own similarly for purposes of recruitment, as well as in-marrying affines on both sides.

The findings we will report are based on only the 1,060 married respondents or 530 couples in our sample. As indicated in the tables below, 416 married people reported siblings along with their siblings' spouses available, while 366 respondents reported spouse's siblings along with their spouses available, and 571 respondents reported adult children along with their spouses.

Ego's Consanguines and Their Spouses

In Table 6-1 we examine recruitment of ego's kindred and their spouses. The table shows whether married couples who are from ego's point of view consanguinal-affinal pairs are seen jointly by respondents and, if they are not, the nature of this imbalance. Table 6-1 arrays these data for ego's collateral kindred and their spouses and intergenerational kindred and their spouses.

The Total column of Table 6-1 shows the proportion of respondents who contacted consanguinal-affinal pairs jointly, separately, and not at all. It reveals that a majority of respondents saw consanguines and affines jointly as a couple, thus supporting the view that the marriage bond is important, and by virtue of this promoting a considerable amount of interaction with affines.

Table 6-1 also shows that this pattern of contacting both consanguines and their spouses jointly extends collaterally and intergenerationally, for the major difference between contacts with siblings and their spouses and adult children and their spouses lies in the fact that siblings and their spouses are less likely than descendants to receive a visit at all. Thus while a majority of respondents'

Table 6-1

Respondents Who Saw Available Consanguines and Consanguine's Spouses Jointly, Separately, or Not at All (In Percentages)

	Collateral Kin Siblings and Siblings' Spouses	Descendant Kin Adult Children and Their Spouses	Total
Respondent saw both consanguines and their spouses	44.5 (185)	76.7 (438)	63.1 (623)
Respondent only saw consanguines	13.0 (54)	9.5 (54)	10.9 (108)
Respondent only saw consanguine's spouse	1.0 (4)	0.0 (0)	.4 (4)
Respondent saw neither	41.6 (173)	13.8 (79)	25.5 (252)
Total	100.0 (416)	100.0 (571)	100.0 (987)

descendants and their spouses are contacted as a couple (76.7 percent), a majority of collaterals are either seen jointly (44.5 percent) as a couple or not at all (41.6 percent). What we found in Chapter 5 pertaining to the husband-wife relation, where a majority of couples saw each other's kindred jointly or not at all, is also in operation in recruitment of consanguinal kin of ego and their spouses. There is symmetry across the husband-wife relation and in recruitment of consanguinal-affinal pairs.

We also find in Table 6-1 that in the minority of cases where consanguinal-affinal pairs are not seen jointly by a respondent, they are not equally likely to be seen. There is clear discrimination along the consanguinal-affinal axis favoring consanguines. While, in general, respondents are unlikely to see affines separately from consanguines, when separate contact does occur it is more likely that consanguines are seen than affines. This pattern extends collaterally to ego's siblings and their spouses as well as intergenerationally to ego's adult children and their spouses. Thus in-marrying affines of ego's consanguines are either seen by respondents jointly with ego's consanguines or not at all. The cultural prescription of treating married people as a couple is reflected in these data as a form of symmetry between kindred and their in-marrying affinal links.

At this stage of our analysis, we cannot assess the relative significance of consanguinal ties as opposed to relations with all affinal kin in a definitive way. However, several points can be made in this regard on the basis of data presented thus far. Commitment to blood ties is in operation in three respects. First, respondents are more likely to see consanguines than affines. A total of 74 percent of our sample saw consanguines (the sum of those who saw both consanguines and their spouses and those who saw only consanguines in the Total column of Table 6-1), compared with about 64 percent who saw affines (the sum of those who saw both consanguines and their spouses and those who saw only consanguine's spouse in the Total column of Table 6-1).

Second, respondents are more likely to see consanguines separately from affines than vice-versa. As Table 6-1 shows, when both siblings and their spouses were available, 13 percent of respondents saw only their siblings, while one percent saw only siblings' spouses. And, while 9.5 percent saw only adult children, none of our respondents saw their children's spouses separately.

Third, the data clearly indicate that ego's consanguines play a role similar to the one we found spouses play in contacting affines (in the preceding chapter). That is, we previously found that respondents contacts with spouse's kindred were contingent on the spouse seeing them. Likewise, contacts with ego's consanguines' in-marrying affines are contingent on ego's contact with consanguines. For affines are not seen unless consanguinal kin (who are the spouses of these affines) are seen as well. Ego's consanguines play an essential intermediary role in ego's contacts with one category of affinal kin—consanguines' spouses.

Ego's Spouse's Consanguines and
Their In-Marrying Affines

It is at this point that we need further information to assess the general significance of consanguinal and affinal ties. So far, we know that consanguines are recruited directly by respondents without intermediary links, but most are seen along with their spouses—who are affines from ego's perspective. So that while more respondents saw consanguines than affines, it is also the case that a majority (63.1 percent in Table 6-1) saw both. However, we do not know whether the pattern of contacts with consanguines and their in-marrying affines are similar to patterns of recruitment of ego's spouse's consanguines and *their* in-marrying affines. The finding that consanguines play a pivotal role for respondents in contacting consanguines' spouses is meaningless without comparable data on the role that other intermediary kin play in this regard.

Our understanding of these issues can be increased in two ways. First, we can determine whether there are different patterns of interaction with ego's consanguines and their spouses than there are with ego's spouse's consanguines and their in-marrying affines. Second, we can clarify the role that intermediary kin play in recruitment. For we must separate the effect that intermediary kin—whether they be ego's consanguines, his spouse, or his affines—have on recruitment from the question of whether these intermediary kin are ego's consanguines or affines.

If consanguinal kin are more important to respondents than affines, then consanguines would be more likely to be seen than any category of affines, regardless of whether these affines are his spouse's consanguines or in-marrying affines of his consanguines or of his spouse, while affines would be less likely to be seen regardless of the kinship role occupied by the intermediary relative providing the connecting link.

In Chapter 5 we found that each spouse plays the pivotal role of an intermediary kinsman who provides a link for ego in his relationship with spouse's kindred. But we also found the recruitment of close and spouse's kindred was balanced by virtue of the fact that they tend to be seen jointly by the couple or not at all. Given the more literal analysis of the role structure of respondent's universe of kin, and the questions posed above, we must return to this data.

We will now explore ego's relationship with his spouse's consanguines and their in-marrying affines in order to examine the effect intermediary kin have on recruitment. Since only one category of kin involved are consanguines (ego's siblings) we will be in a better position to assess the significance of affinal and consanguinal ties. First, we will examine married couples' recruitment of their own siblings and spouse's siblings. This data is presented in Table 6-2 and shows whether or not siblings and spouse's siblings are equally likely to be seen, as well as the role each respondent plays in providing a link between his or her spouse

Table 6-2
Married Couples Who Saw Available Siblings and Spouse's Siblings Jointly and Separately (In Percentages)

	Husband's Siblings	Wife's Siblings
Both husband and wife saw	42.6	56.2
Only husband saw	8.5	2.8
Only wife saw	2.2	7.5
Neither saw	46.6	33.5
Total	100.0	100.0
	(233)	(281)

and consanguines. Second, we will examine ego's recruitment of his spouse's siblings and their in-marrying affines. This data (presented in Table 6-3) shows whether or not there is symmetry in recruitment of these affinal couples as well as the role ego's spouse's consanguines play in this regard. This will permit us to separate the question of the effects intermediary kin have on recruitment from the question of whether these intermediary kin are ego's consanguines or affines.

Table 6-2 shows whether the siblings of the husband and wife are seen jointly, separately by either husband or wife, or not at all. In it we find that when siblings are seen separately, the husband is more likely to see his own siblings and the wife is more likely to see her siblings than either of them to see their spouse's siblings. The proportionate difference between husbands and wives is not at issue here, and was discussed in Chapter 5. What is important is the interpretive value these findings have for the role spouses play as linkages with their respective consanguines. There is a clear indication that each spouse serves as a pivotal connecting link between their consanguines and his or her own marital partner. For the great majority of these couples, the siblings of each spouse are seen either by the conjugal pair jointly or not at all; and when siblings are seen separately, each respondent is more likely to see their own siblings rather than either of them seeing their spouse's siblings.

We cannot overestimate the important role that each spouse plays in this regard. We have previously found that when this conjugal link is missing through the disruptions in marriage, so too is the continuity in relationships with ego's spouse's kindred. But as long as the marriage is intact, there is balance across the husband-wife axis and equal treatment of their respective consanguines in interaction terms.

To further clarify the relative significance of consanguinal and affinal kin and the role intermediary kin play in recruitment, we turn from the analysis of husband-wife linkages with their consanguines to respondents' recruitment of

Table 6-3

Respondents Who Saw Available Spouse's Siblings and Spouse's Siblings' Spouses Jointly, Separately, or Not at All (In Percentages)

	Spouse's Siblings and Spouse's Siblings' Spouses
Respondent saw both spouse's siblings and spouse's siblings' spouses	40.7
Respondent only saw spouse's siblings	11.5
Respondent only saw spouse's siblings' spouses	1.9
Respondent saw neither	45.9
Total	100.0
	(366)

affinal couples—spouse's siblings and spouse's siblings' spouses. Our specific concern is to assess the role that ego's spouse's siblings play in recruitment of *their* spouses as well as to determine the extent of symmetry occurring in recruitment of these affinal couples. These data are presented in Table 6-3.

Table 6-3 shows that a similar pattern is found in recruitment of totally affinal couples' spouse's siblings and their in-marrying affines as was found in recruitment of ego's siblings and their in-marrying affines (shown in Table 6-1). A majority of affinal couples are contacted jointly or not at all; thus, regardless of whether kin are ego's consanguines and their spouses or spouse's consanguines and *their* spouses, we find these respondents contacting married people jointly as a couple—the difference being that ego's spouse serves as an intermediary between himself and his spouse's siblings and their spouses, where no such intermediary exists in recruitment of ego's own siblings.

We also find in Table 6-3 that the same directionality of imbalances that occur in recruitment of consanguinal kin and their spouses is in operation in recruitment of totally affinal couples. When affinal couples are not seen jointly by respondents they are also not equally likely to be seen. Respondents are more likely to see spouse's siblings separately than they are to see spouse's siblings' spouses. That is, it is more likely that spouse's consanguines are seen separately than are their in-marrying affines. This inequality, however, is not due to consanguinity from the point of view of ego. Hence it is not blood that makes these ties more important in interaction terms; rather it would appear to be norms applying to ego's spouse in maintaining ties with her consanguines and norms applying to ego to visit his spouse's consanguines that accounts for this differential.

Since we found in Table 6-2 that respondents see spouse's siblings only when their spouses see them, and since Table 6-3 shows that respondents are unlikely to see spouse's siblings' spouses without also seeing spouse's siblings, we must conclude that ego's interaction with both these categories of affines is dependent on his spouse's, who provides the necessary link. Contact with these affinal couples depends not only on the extent to which ego's spouse promotes relations with siblings but also on the extent to which ego's spouse's siblings provide a link with their own in-marrying affines.

In summary, we find the cultural emphasis on the marital relation as a solidary one reflected in recruitment of relatives as couples. This pattern holds for all kin who are married, regardless of whether they are consanguines or affines. This aspect of kin interaction is symmetrical within all husband-wife pairs, yet at the same time is contingent on ego's relationships with intermediary kin who provide the necessary pivotal link between his affines and himself. For in the absence of contact with intermediary kin, in-marrying affines of ego's kindred and those of his spouse's are not seen. And as we have noted, in the absence of ego's spouse, an entire segment of his universe of kin are not seen.

In addition to the symmetry in contact with couples, we find that contact with ego's consanguines and spouse's consanguines is balanced across the husband-wife axis, and at the same time contingent on ego and his spouse's willingness or ability to provide the link between the consanguinal kin and his or her spouse. The balancing effect is also brought about by cultural norms emphasizing joint visiting of kin by respondents and their spouses.

The difference in recruitment of ego's own consanguines and their spouses and the recruitment of ego's spouse's consanguines and their spouses is this: Ego has a choice in contacting his own consanguines that does not exist in contacts with spouse's consanguines, as this decision is a matter for ego's spouse to make, not ego. However, beyond this balanced dimension of recruitment, we find that recruitment of other affines—in particular siblings' spouses and spouse's siblings' spouses—is contingent on focal intermediary kin who provide the connecting link. To speak of ego's choice in seeing these kin is meaningless since it is intermediary kin who provide the link and hence "make the choice" of whether ego will see them.

The Kindred-Based Linkage Model

Consanguinity and marriage are the basic facts of the culture of kinship in any society. But in our own, both also assume a prominent role in determining how the relational system operates.

The bilateral reckoning of consanguinity contributes to the absence of any corporate kin groups other than the household, and brings into preeminence a category of kin Rivers (1924) identified as kindred. As Freeman (1961:209) points out, kindred relations are governed by a special morality arising from the recognition of common descent. This morality accounts for one normative aspect of extra-familial kin ties in the United States.

The social recognition of consanguinity affixes a particular quality to the social interaction of kin which is distinct from all other relationships in our society because it is preordained. The *a priori* existence of this kinship bond establishes the possibility that individuals may promote social relations with kindred with minimal effort. It is in this sense that Freeman's claim (1961:211)—that the kindred presents the individual with a wide range of relationships which, in the absence of any binding descent principle, it is possible for an individual to accentuate as he pleases or as suits his special interests—must be understood. For she is not stating that relations among kindred lack norms, or are based on idiosyncratic factors, or are universally matters of individual choice only. In fact, she not only claims (1961:210) that obligations among kindred exist but that degrees of gradation in obligations within the kindred are usual, often varying with closeness of consanguinity and the generation of those concerned. Her point is that while kindred relations are not necessarily *dominated* by this notion of gradation, it is nevertheless present. It is by virtue of the common recognition of descent that kindred admit a special obligation toward one another: an obligation to give help and support in culturally determined ways (Freeman: 1961:209).

Thus it may be said that it is the preordained character of kindred relations that is of fundamental importance in the operation of the system of kinship interaction in the United States. And, it is the morality arising from this characteristic that accounts for the existence of kinship norms.

But social relations among affines lack this characteristic. For no *a priori* relation exists between affines; and to treat kindred and affinal relations as equivalent is to obscure this essential analytic and empirical distinction. Based as they are upon connecting kindred, spouses, and spouses' kindred, relations among affines cannot be as readily mobilized. The cessation of interaction not only hinges on ego's relationship with this relative, but on ego's relationship with his own kindred, or his spouse's kindred, or these relatives' relationship with affines.

Hence to speak of ego's choice in recruitment for interaction is meaningless, as we have said, with respect to affines. The innumerable intermediary connecting links would seem to mitigate against any direct appeal for help or aid. Thus to speak of kinship norms (as distinct from marital norms) with respect to affines is irrelevant in terms of the actual recruitment of these kin for interaction.

However, it must be clearly emphasized that to claim that relations among affines are different and lack a normative kinship base is not to say that they are less important. This is particularly evident in our own society, where emphasis is placed on the marital bond. In fact, it is the normative emphasis on the marital relations and not the ascribed, or perhaps quasi-ascribed, status of being an affine which is of primary importance in understanding patterns of recruitment of these kin. For it is the normative demands placed on the marital relation—and not a special system of kin norms applying to affines—that account for the affinal dimension of the pattern of kinship interaction.

Not only is the system of monogamous marriage more important in understanding relations among kin than was previously thought, but as Parsons (1943:33) has seen, it interacts with the kinship system in such a way as to place a premium on both husband and wife in maintaining ties with their respective kindred. This emphasis on the marriage relation as a solidary one has created a system of pivotal linkages between kindreds.

The principal structural relation between separate kindreds is based on the fact that each spouse is expected to play a pivotal role in maintaining contact with their own kindred. It is precisely these norms placed on married couples that lead to the conclusion that social relations among relatives in our society are kindred-based rather than resting wholly on the kindred itself.

In our society, then, the core of the relational system of kinship is constituted by focal egos and their socially significant kindred and affines. The category of relatives directly connected to ego and on whom he primarily depends are his bilateral kin or kindred. In addition, the marriage of ego and also the marriages of his kindred create three other categories of affines, which may be described as follows: (1) on ego's side there are ego's kindred's spouses' kindred; on his wife's side there are (2) his spouse's kindred; and also on his wife's side there are (3) the kindred of ego's spouse's kindred's spouses.

Each member of ego's own kindred forms a connecting link for ego with his or her spouse and that spouse's kindred. These kindred—who are in-marrying affines of ego's kindred—form a final link with their spouses and kindred—which we have not and will not discuss.

The most significant fact of the relational system is the individual's lack of dependence on any kin grouping for establishing or maintaining kinship relations, and a total dependence on focal relatives, ego himself, and the pivotal role of intermediary kin: representatives of his kindred, his spouse's kindred and so on. The underlying basis for recruitment of kin for interaction, then, is the extent to which ego and intermediary kin provide the opportunity for social relationships among relatives.

Seen from a somewhat more generalized point of view, if we take the category of ego's relatives (known as kindred) as a system, we find that it can be, but is not necessarily, articulated with a series of distinct kindred by the marriages of each member of the kindred. The consequence of such linkages is to maximize the opportunity for social relationships with a large number of people while at the same time preventing the formation of kinship *groups* other than the household.

And if we assume ego is married, the kindred of each spouse operates as two systems which provide the opportunity for a very large number of social relations being established on a kinship basis but with a minimum of demands placed on husband or wife. Given the solidary emphasis on the conjugal relation in our society and the dislocations of kindreds resulting from geographic mobility, one can easily see how Parsons' cultural analysis of American kinship led him to the broad historical conclusion that the household was isolated from kin and the isolated nuclear family was the central fact of kinship in this society. But in point of fact, the nuclear family is merely the only concrete group formed on the basis of kinship so long as its members reside in the same household: this still leaves the entire universe of kinship interaction to be accounted for. Parsons deals only with kinship groups and fails to deal with kinship interaction. Isolation with respect to the former does not, of course, mean isolation exists with respect to the latter.

Recognizing that families nevertheless were related by blood collaterally and generationally, Parsons (1943:24) portrayed the system as made up exclusively of a series of interlocking nuclear families. However, Parsons did not try to specify the mechanism relating these families to one another and thus failed to see not only how the relational system of kinship operated, but also that the term interlocking is itself a misnomer when applied to interaction because it is kindred which are linked, and not interlocked. In terms of interaction it is irrelevant in principle whether or not these are household units, for the simple reason that concrete groups of kin are trivial in terms of the actual interaction of relatives. The household is the *only* concrete kin grouping in American society; it is not isolated in kinship interaction terms because it is unique.

Social interaction patterns among kin in the working class are then best analyzed by a kindred-based model that has been modified by certain features of an urban-industrial mode of life, fragmenting the kindred on a locality basis, and by the structural premium placed on the marital bond.

The relational system is kindred-based and linked with other kindred through marriages. The linkages among kindred are balanced on either side of ego's affinal line—and, moreover, across all affinal lines of all kin, consanguinal or not by conjugal norms. The relational model of kinship in the United States is thus kindred-based, linked with other kindred through affines, and balanced across all lines by conjugal norms.

Conclusion

In this chapter we have come to the end of our analysis of data on kinship interaction. It is appropriate, then, to briefly review our starting point and survey some of the findings and the points of view we have developed insofar as they may provide a context for better understanding the significance of the conclusions to be made on the basis of this chapter.

In the first chapter we posed the problem of kinship in terms of an ego-centered approach. In the ensuing chapters we attempted to establish that by using this approach rather than the household approach (with proper precautions), the analysis of behavior among extra-familial kin is more fruitful—given that the kindred is a common structural component in societies with bilateral descent. Our goal has been to explain the problem of variability in kinship behavior by discovering the organizational principles operative in these working class individuals' interaction with their kin and affines.

Let us assess where we stand with respect to that goal, and then evaluate the extent to which our approach has more value for the clarification of data on extra-familial kin ties than other models currently in use, notably Sussman's kin network and Litwak's modified extended family.

Litwak's and Sussman's research has obscured the basic fact that variability in kinship behavior is systematic and is manifested in specific ways. In their attempt to identify a unit of kinship outside the domestic group, they have used concepts suggesting a group of an unspecified—perhaps varying—number of relatives who have some form of expected interaction with one another, if not overlapping ties, duties, and rights. It is not clear which kinship roles comprise this grouping of kin; nor do we know the contexts in which these relatives do and do not participate in social relations. And, contrary to these authors' explicit and implied claims, their data fails to show that these kin necessarily do form groups.

It is the issue of *which* kinship roles are generally implicated in social relations among kin, and thus may be considered socially effective, that raises the overall question of the utility of the Sussman and Litwak conceptions. The ego-centered approach used throughout this study points to differences between people at various stages of the life cycle and between spouses in the extent of contact with various categories of relatives that we have characterized as kindred types. Since an individual's position in the life cycle determines the identify of his socially effective kin, "kin network" and "modified extended family" become vague referents to the existence of ongoing social relationships with kin not living in the same household.

Our data clearly indicate that the composition of the kin network and modified extended family must change over time. We have found that factors such as age and marital status are related to the extent of contact with various kindred types, thus the Sussman and Litwak approaches simply do not permit an analysis of this problem.

Ego-centered analysis alone, however, cannot bring out what is distinctive about relations among kin in our society, because characteristics of our kinship system play an essential role in this regard. Bilateral kinship systems generally lack any kin group outside the household unit: the unit of kinship other than the household, which has been found in societies such as these, is the kindred. The kindred is not a group but rather an ego-centered category of socially significant blood relatives. In the absence of large kinship groups, and with the reckoning of descent on both the maternal and paternal side, the kindred provides an individual with a large number of relatives with whom he may establish and maintain social relationships.

Given these considerations, the role that our kinship system plays in interaction has not been brought out in previous studies. We have found, however, that ordering of recruitment of kindred types reflects these priorities of our kinship system. The finding that factors extraneous to kinship place constraints on behavior among kin, yet are *not* determinative of who will be seen, is of crucial significance. It suggests that the structure of kin ties can be stretched by the special conditions of our industrial-urban mode of life, but not so far as to lack any identity at all. Here again we find that previous work has neglected or obscured this basic fact.

Thus along with other studies we have found that the geographical dispersion of kin throughout the society leaves the individual with a fragmented kindred on a locality basis. However, what is significant is that dispersion or lack of it does not affect the patterning of recruitment of available kindred types. And the geographical dispersion of kin within the metropolitan area does not affect the priorities in recruitment of kindred types.

The persistence of interaction patterns across kindred types raises another question. It will be recalled from Chapter 3 that the terms in which kinship relations are described in the literature are diverse and indicate opposing views. While some authors such as Reiss and Adams have stressed the importance of genealogical distance as a basis for kinship interaction, others such as Mogey and Cumming and Schneider have stressed equalitarian norms that permitted kin to be selected on nonkinship bases. In fact, it appeared that the kin ties these various authors were talking about were simply of a different sort. But they were not. All had in mind the same referent—the structure of kin ties extending beyond the household. Since we are talking about the same thing, the issue remains: what is the nature of the norms governing extra-familial kin ties in the United States?

In Chapter 3, we refuted the thesis that this structure is such that kin are treated as a body in obligation terms (as inferred from the modified extended family construct) and also rejected the notion that the structure is so loose as to lack any identity at all. Moreover, we examined the kinds of norms governing kinship relations and the extent to which they were obligatory or permissive. We refuted a major dimension of the "equalitarian thesis" of selecting kin for interaction and implied the existence of specific kinship norms as manifested in our respondents' behavior towards their kin. We found that in terms of ego's own kindred, his joint descendants were the first order of priority in recruitment since more of them were seen more frequently than any other category of kindred. Close kindred occupied a second position, along with spouse's kindred, and distant kindred followed.

On the basis of evidence presented since that chapter, some of the issues regarding the nature of the relational system of kinship require further clarification. In Chapter 5 we found that the symmetry in recruitment of close kindred and spouse's among married couples exists only if both husband and wife are willing and able to play a pivotal role in contacting their own kindred; while in Chapter 4 we found that recruitment of close kindred and spouse's kindred among the not married is asymmetrical, with the emphasis on close kindred. These findings, together with those pointing to variability in contact with certain kindred types by age, raise anew the question of the meaning of choice, opportunity, and constraint in recruitment of kin. Data such as these seriously challenge the view promoted by Cumming, Schneider, and others that individuals in our society exercise a great deal of choice in selecting which kin they will see.

We have contended that kinship norms governing interaction are in fact operant in our society. But this statement must be properly understood. We are rejecting the claim that kin relations are totally permissive and that individuals consequently exercise a great deal of choice of which relatives they see—our data disprove this. This interpretation of choice rests on the assumption that there exists an undifferentiated relational system of kinship; whereas, what we actually have is a system differentiated by kinship connections within which there exist priorities in recruitment. The assumption of an undifferentiated system is a denial that kinship considerations play an important role in determining which relatives are seen. We have found this not to be so. The meaning of individual choice interaction must be reconsidered in light of the role that kinship plays.

Thus, while every individual has the choice of treating some relatives and not others with particular consideration—and while this selectivity may well depend to some extent on his own needs, special interests, and the like—the choice of the relative will also be influenced by the cultural system of kinship that specifies their genealogical relation with each other. But the context in which *choice* may be said to be the criterion of kinship interaction should be clearly understood. This term can only be used to describe kinship relations in a legitimate sense if one thinks of it in contrast to customary obligations. In other words, it is in comparison with unilineal systems of kinship, where overriding corporate kin obligations exist, that choice can be said to characterize kinship relations in bilateral descent systems.

It is only in this comparative perspective that "choice" makes sense in understanding our kinship system. Choice does not mean the absence of structure, although it does suggest the absence of corporate kin groups. The concept provides a means of analyzing relationships among kin. As Lancaster (1961:324) has noted in this context, choice must always be considered in the light of the strength of sanctions that bear on ego. From this perspective, we would suggest that while some kin ties can be characterized by a set of duties and obligations, others may not. In some cases, individuals may or may not decide to establish or continue a social relationship on the basis of a recognized kinship tie. Clearly the type of kindred the relative represents, and thus the strength of sanctions bearing on ego, come into play in this regard. It is simply not a matter of ego's whim or fancy but one of kinship that decides the strength with which these norms operate.

Thus we do not concur with Schneider's view that a relative is first of all a person and that other characteristics of his status-set are more important than the kinship bond in forming a social relationship with a relative. This view assumes the absence of kinship norms and suggests that kin ties are indistinguishable from relations among neighbors and friends. Kin ties *are* different. They may even have a definite advantage over nonkin ties, such as friendship, for in many situations the individual may rely on the sanctions of kin norms which simply do not exist in the same form as those of friendship. The issue here is not the existence or nonexistence of kinship and friendship norms per se, but the extent to which they differ. Our point is that kinship norms differ from those of friendship and that it is a mistake to confuse the two, as Schneider seems to have done.

Moreover, the norms that are operative in extra-familial kin ties cannot be seen developing within the family. As Freeman (1961:209) has pointed out, the norms of kinship are not simple extensions of sentiments developed in the nuclear family but are rooted in the kinship system in which the family and kin ties are embedded. Thus we must reject Parsons' (1968:38) attempt to reconcile his own view on isolation from kin with the findings of others, wherein he claims that social relations among kin outside the nuclear family household are not broken because of the psychological importance of the individual's own family of orientation in which he was born and brought up.

Parsons is suggesting that the relational system of American kinship is a reflection of sentiments developed in the family and thus is temporally a product of the social synchronization achieved in the process of socialization. While consistent with his view of the effects of industrialization on kin groups, this quasi-socialization theory does not account for the relational system as we have thus far found it. It thus appears that Parsons has attempted to account for the *origins* of feelings which may—but not necessarily do—provide a basis for social relationships among consanguinal kin.

This view fails to account for such differences as we found in contact between collateral and descendant kindred, while totally ignoring the entire universe of kinship made up by affines. Relational norms of kinship, rooted as they are in the entire kinship system, come into existence in the same manner as do those governing the family—by the interplay between the kinship system and other societal subsystems. In attempting to reconcile his own theory in the light of new data, Parsons has muddled his own contribution to the field.

It may appear that in rejecting some aspects of the views of Schneider, Parsons, Litwak, and Sussman, we have unfairly criticized the perhaps careless use of terms. But this is not so; they mean precisely what they say. Litwak and Sussman do in fact point to a group-based structure of kin ties, which they have vastly overrated in terms of functionality and pervasiveness. And Schneider and

Parsons attempt to refute the existence of specific kinship norms. Such formulations are misleading. We have posed anew the problem of extra-familial kin ties because neither one of these two opposing conceptualizations of kinship reflects the underlying bases on which kin are selected for interaction.

Thus we finally come to the conclusions one may draw on the basis of this chapter: the recognition of common descent provides the normative basis for extra-familial kin ties in the United States. These norms only apply to common descendants who from ego's point of view are his kindred. The preordained and *a priori* relation among kindred has no counterpart among affines, whether they are related to ego by virtue of the marriages of his kindred, himself, or his spouse's kindred. Thus to speak of kinship norms among affines is a misnomer, and to suggest that kinship norms apply equally to consanguines and affines is erroneous.

The moral basis of extra-familial kin ties has been extended in our society by marriage norms. It is in this way that the affinal dimension of American kinship can be understood, for it is by virtue of the expectation that the kindred of both husband and wife be treated equally in interaction terms that relations among affines are made important in our society.

Consanguinal and affinal kin are equally important to respondents as long as marriages remain intact; not because the norms of kinship apply equally to both, but by virtue of the fact that conjugal norms are equally important and, hence, have sanctioning power equal to norms of the kindred. This fact is reflected in the pattern of joint visiting of married couples with their respective kindred, as well as respondents contacting consanguinal-affinal pairs jointly. It is conjugal norms which account for the balancing of linkages among different kindred.

While the research of the past two decades shows that individuals often have social relations with various categories of relatives, little else was known. The data did not show that kin formed groups, as implied by Sussman and Litwak. And no evidence exists showing how membership in such a group could or would be defined. The attribution of group-like qualities to patterns of kinship interaction goes far beyond any legitimate inference that can be made from known data.

Our own data show that it is likely that some of ego's socially significant kin (however defined) neither know one another nor would interact with one another if they did. Some kin are connected directly to ego (his kindred) while others are more tenuously connected (affines) through various intermediaries such as his spouse, his siblings, and his adult children. To proclaim that these analytically separate categories of relatives form a "network" or "group" of kin is simply to force data into meaningless and useless conceptual models.

We have thus superseded the limited work of Sussman and Litwak by developing a model that has value for the clarification of data on extra-familial kin ties. The kindred-based linkage model we propose differs fundamentally from the "kin network" and "modified extended family." It does not assume that group properties attach to kin relation. It is ego-centered—depending for its very existence on a specific person. This ego focus makes no assumption regarding kin groups, and since there are no assumptions about groups, the model permits the inclusion of relatives, regardless of why they contact—or even know—ego's other relatives.

The most significant fact that our model points to is the individual's lack of dependence on any kin grouping for establishing or maintaining kinship relations, and an almost total dependence on focal relatives—ego himself, and the intermediary role of focal kin: his spouse's kindred, his kindred and so on. The underlying basis for recruitment of kin for interaction, then, is the extent to which ego and his intermediary kin provide the opportunity for social relationships among relatives. The research issue is to account for factors that promote and do not promote ego and his intermediary kin to provide these opportunities.

We submit that the recognition of common descent provides the normative basis for kinship interaction among kindred. Affines are a different matter. While Schneider (1968:80-92) acknowledged that relationships with inlaws are not as binding as relationships with one's own kindred as reflected in kinship reckoning, he failed to specify why this was so. We suggest that kinship norms governing consanguinal kindred do not pertain to affines, but rather that affinal relations are governed by marriage norms. Thus the emphasis on the conjugal bond as a solidary one results in norms specifying joint visiting of the kindred of both husband and wife; and these same conjugal norms provide the sole basis on which relationships with affines are initiated and sustained. Therefore, the relational system of kinship is kindred-based and balanced through linkages with affines.

7

Kinship and Social Structure

In this final chapter it is appropriate to present a synoptic view of the relational system of kinship as it has emerged in the foregoing analysis and then to consider some of the larger implications of these findings in a speculative and interpretive way.

The Relational System of Kinship

In the first place, we have found that the availability of relatives in the metropolitan Philadelphia area places limitations on the kinship groupings which can be realized in interaction of a common, repetitive, everyday nature. While almost everyone possesses among their pool of available relatives some who at one time had lived in their household as nuclear family members (close and joint descendant kindred), it is nevertheless not possible for more than about 30 percent of the sample to interact with two generations of such kin because representatives of *both* close and joint descendant kin are present in the metropolitan area for no greater proportion of the sample than this. Put another way, lack of propinquity rules out the interlocking, on the basis of repetitive interaction, of nuclear family units over two generations for most working class people. Again, considering the bilateral kindred as a unit of kinship interaction, it is true that very few people lack any representatives of close, distant, or joint descendant kin in the area. But no more than 20 percent of the sample can report the presence of at least one relative from each kindred type comprising a complete bilateral kindred. Considering the lateral kinship configuration of close and spouse's kindred as a unit of interaction, less than a third of these working class people have even one representative of both these kindred types living in the metropolitan area. And if one looks at all the kindred types delineated here for purposes of analysis of kinship interaction, only about 12 percent of these working class Philadelphians have a relative from all four kindred types in the area.

It is clear, then, that the opportunity structure of kinship interaction is indistinct and fragmented, and that sheer availability does not weight the selection of kin for interaction in any particular direction. Judging from the one comparable study of the availability of middle class people's kin, the same situation prevails in other levels of the socioeconomic hierarchy.

Taking into account the distribution of available relatives over the four kindred types delineated in this study, we find a characteristic pattern of interaction that neither wholly conforms to the ideas of those who state that the recruitment of kin is a matter of relatively free choice on the part of any given ego (i.e., that it is based on equalitarian criteria) nor to the ideas of those who assert that relations of consanguinity and genealogical distance serve as the criteria for kinship interaction. Both these principles of recruitment appear to be involved in different and particular ways in kinship interaction.

The principle of consanguinity manifests itself in an invariant order of precedence in interaction. More representatives of joint descendant kindred are recruited by a larger proportion of respondents for whom such kinship roles are available, and they are seen more frequently than any other type of kindred. Second in order of precedence come close and spouse's kindred, occupying about the same rank—(they are composed of genealogically parallel kinship roles on either side of the affinal line). Distant kindred rank last in terms of kinship interaction.

That this ordering is indeed based on norms of kinship is seen in the patterning of interaction under different conditions of availability of genealogically important kindred types such as joint descendants and close kindred and less important types such as distant kindred. When the more and the less important kindred types are available, those of least kinship importance may not be seen, or few may see them. If kindred types of greatest importance are not available, but those of least importance are, no kin may be seen in preference to contacting those of least importance—there being no compensation for lack of availability through contacting those relatives who are present. But when a wider variety of kindred types exist in the area, then a more varied set of kin may be recruited for interaction, with the emphasis on the genealogically more important types as indicated.

It is apparent that this order of priority in recruitment of kin for interaction conforms closely with the bilaterality of our kinship structure. Thus it is not unexpected that most emphasis is placed on the joint issue of both lines of descent (and equally so for the representatives of each line). Also, it is precisely in conformity with the bilateral nature of kinship that the genealogically close relatives of the representatives of both lines should be recruited equally in frequency and extent, and rank next in order of importance. Lower priority, of course, is assigned to the more distant kin.

But to focus on the kinship norms involved in ordering priorities of recruitment of relatives for interaction is not to deny any role to so called equalitarian criteria of kinship interaction. Geographical distance between relatives serves as one such criterion, of a nonkinship sort. The effect of distance is marked: it is highly negatively associated with the level of interaction with kin. But the effect of distance applies uniformly to interaction with every kindred type. The result is that the overall level at which the relational system of kinship operates is reduced by distance while the order of priority by which kin are recruited for interaction remains the same. The effect of nonkinship criteria, then, is to dampen rather than distort the pattern of kinship interaction. It does not appear that those theories claiming the importance of nonkinship factors on kinship qua kinship interaction have any essential validity. At best such factors simply condition the operation of the kinship norms involved.

The failure of geographical distance to reorder kinship priorities is not an idiosyncratic effect. Another fundamental variable, of a nonkinship nature, also fails to upset the pattern of kinship interaction. This is the stage of the life cycle at which an individual has arrived, as indexed by age. At all ages, within the considerable age range of our sample, regardless of geographical distance and regardless of the dimension of kinship interaction measured, and controlling for availability, the order of kinship precedence in interaction remains the same. Joint descendant kindred are seen most, close and spouse's kindred together rank next, and distant kindred follow the rest. Like geographical distance, stage of life cycle (as indicated by age) conditions the level of interaction occurring among kin without distorting the patterned order of interaction. However, as with geographical distance, the role of life cycle stage in the level of interaction is also of inherent interest. Thus, while the order of precedence in kinship interaction is preserved, younger people interact more, in general, with kin than older people.

The aged are not the foci of urban kin relations, despite the claims of Adams, on the basis of the criteria employed here. In addition, it does not appear that close kindred become important sources of socioemotional interaction in later stages of the life cycle, as Cumming and Schneider claim. Instead, Young and Wilmott's view that relationships with these kin generally become attenuated in the later stages of life appears to be confirmed. But none of these students of kinship has noticed the crucial role played by termination of the conjugal relationship occurring at late stages of the life cycle.

Age does not, for example, erode the relationships of the widowed, divorced or separated with their close kindred nearly to the extent that it does among people who are still married. As long as the marriage remains intact, the normative pattern of treating close and spouse's kindred equally for interaction also prevails. But when in the late stages of the life cycle marriages are disrupted, former spouse's kindred are not subjectively considered as kin by most survivors of the union, and interaction with close kindred is stressed.

During the years in which the marriage is intact, however, the interaction of a marital partner with his or her own close kindred and spouse's kindred takes a particular form, that of a system of balanced linkages. For both husband and wife play a pivotal role in providing linkages to interaction with their respective close kindred. If the husband does not see his close kindred, his wife will not see them; if the wife does not see her close kindred, her husband will not see them. When close kindred are seen, they are either contacted by both husband and wife or by the spouse for whom they are close kindred. Thus women do not act as representatives of the domestic unit in contacting relatives; they do not play the pivotal role in interaction with kin that Adams and Robins and Tomanec would have them do.

Moreover, there is no evidence of a matricentric bias, strictly speaking, in kinship interaction. That is, it is not the case that the wife fails to fulfill her obligations to contact her husband's kin, but rather that the husband fails to provide the necessary linkage with his close kindred. When the husband does provide this link, wives also contact his consanguines. Likewise, husbands are not drawn into interaction with their wives' kindred to the neglect of their own, but rather accompany their wives when their wives see their own kindred. Simply put, one reason wives do not see their husbands' kindred is that their husbands are not seeing them. Husbands, on the other hand, are seeing their wives' close kindred because their wives see them.

But there are other reasons why wives may have greater involvement with their close kindred. One of these is the age difference between spouses. The differential between spouses in contacting their respective close kindred is considerably reduced by holding age constant. Older people's contact with kin is attenuated, and husbands are older than their wives. Since kindred are mainly seen jointly, the age differences between husbands and wives means that husbands with younger wives see their wives' close kindred because these younger women are more likely to see their close kindred. The so-called matricentric bias is misleadingly termed, for it is not a function of kinship per se, but is rather an artifact of age differences in the conjugal pair as they influence the balanced linkages of interaction across the affinal line.

In addition to age, the internal dynamics of the marriage are involved in tipping the equal balance of interaction. Highly segregated conjugal role relationships are associated with constraints on joint interaction of the married couple with relatives and constraints on seeing spouse's kindred for both husband and wife. Or, said differently, the sharing of domestic activities makes it more likely that husband and wife will participate as a couple in activities outside the household.

Both age and conjugal role segregation have only an indirect relation to kinship qua kinship. By taking account of them, the level of what has been termed matricentricity is reduced. These factors, essentially extraneous to kinship, are responsible for departures from culturally prescribed patterns of behavior—in this case the normative prescript of equal treatment of the kindred of each spouse in social relations.

Beyond the issue of matricentricity, the nature of the lateral extension of kinship interaction in general assumes primary importance in the relational system of kinship. Indeed, consanguinal and affinal kin are equally recruited unless the conjugal pair is broken up. But this is not because the norms governing consanguineal kindred also govern affines. Rather, the marital norms governing the husband and wife are as important as those governing consanguinal kindred. Conjugal norms account for the balancing of linkages among different kindred—which is demonstrated by the particular pattern of joint visiting by married couples with their respective kindred, as well as the way in which each husband or wife contacts consanguinal-affinal pairs among his or her kindred. This is the major feature of the relational model of kinship interaction in the working class, and also, we would strongly suggest, in American society at large.

Single-Core or Plural Kinship System

It is evident from the nature of the relational system of kinship we have described that the unit of working class kinship (and also, we maintain, of American kinship) is the kindred. We refer here to the entire bilateral kindred of course, but mainly to the subtypes we have termed joint descendant, close, spouse's, and distant kindred. The variability in kinship relations we have described throughout this book cannot be accounted for, much less be described, in terms of elementary (nuclear) families. Nor can this variability be understood in terms of a putative extended kinship group, modified or otherwise. Kindreds do not and cannot form groups. Yet, as we have seen, kindreds are not thereby merely conglomerations of statuses defined by rules of kinship nomenclature. They are functioning aggregates, formed on the basis kinship norms by ego's patterns of interaction; and they refer to ego in his capacity as a relative, not to kinship networks as constituted of concrete groups of relatives.

Because bilateral systems of kinship do not as a rule generate formal groups of kin, and because the domestic unit by contrast stands out as the one observable kinship entity having any group characteristics, the sociological response to the vacuum left by the lack of attention paid to bilateral kinship systems by anthropologists (until only recently) has been to oscillate between two extremes of conceptualization. Either no structured kinship entities but isolated elementary households were discerned, or else extended kin groupings of a dubious nature were alleged to exist—and on the basis of unconvincing (Gibson, 1972) evidence, moreover.

But the implication of our description of the relational system of kinship is that the kindred and kindred types are principles of organization and function-ing entities of kinship which are neither concrete groups organized along extra-familial lines nor cultural aspects of kinship which lack relational signifi-cance in concrete patterns of kinship interaction. The kindred is obviously an adaptable and flexibile unit of kinship.

What emerges, then, from the preceding chapters of this book is that the kindred is so adaptable that it can be—and often is—mistaken for plural kinship systems. Contemporary instances of this tendency are to be found in the culture of poverty thesis, in some assessments of the significance of female-headed families among blacks (and in the working class matricentricity thesis in general), and in the work of those who attribute to the elite of wealth a kinship structure characterized by lineage-like elements.

But perhaps it would be best to go to the intellectual source of speculations such as these. Parsons (1943:28-29), in a fundamental misunderstanding of the structure of bilateral kinship systems for which the state of anthropology and sociology of the 1940s are as much to blame as he is, mentions that the incidence of the fully developed kinship type "... in the American social structure is uneven and important tendencies to deviation from it are found in certain structural areas." He then goes on to cite the social location of three exceptions to the focal type of kinship organization: (1) solidly established rural populations; (2) parts of the upper class; and (3) parts of the lower class, black as well as white. In the latter instance, he characterizes the deviation from the norm as a "mother-centered" type of family structure, coupled with a strong tendency toward the instability of marriage.

We now know that the adaptability of kindreds in bilateral kinship systems does not mean a variant from some focal kinship emphasis has occurred. It is in the nature of kindred-based systems of kinship not to be disintegrated by the departure of one of the conjugal pair from the domiciliary unit. The household is not the unit of kinship of bilateral systems, even though it may be a feature of them. The system is quite flexible enough to adjust to this circumstance without transforming into something else.

In view of the analysis of the preceding chapters it would not make any sense to say, for example, that there was a strong tendency toward the instability of marriage because many are left widowed in old age. Yet from the point of view of the system, there is no essential difference here between the economic pressures that compel lower class males to move from their households and the emptying of the households of the aged by death, or the households of those of any age by divorce or separation. Members of bilateral kinship systems belong to what we have termed their close kindred before *and* after their marriages are disrupted—whatever the reasons for the disruption.

We have seen that the kindred-based system continues to function flexibly when members of our sample are widowed, divorced, or separated. Former spouse's kindred are not considered relatives any longer, by and large, and compensatory interaction with close kindred takes place. This extra utilization of close kindred by those whose marriages have dissolved exceeds the norm for others of the same age whose marriages remain intact.

This pattern of adaptability of kindreds is hardly a deviation from the main kinship mode. It is the way the modal kinship system itself works. The fact that marriages are disrupted, by economic hardship or by death, is not a function of kinship; it is a function of systems to which kinship stands in some overlapping or boundary relation. Thus the implication that there is a significant social class deviation from the modal kinship system can only be rejected on the basis of such evidence. The disruption of marriage occurs in all classes and for a variety of reasons. When this happens, the conjugal survivor does not perforce "leave the system." For the unit of kinship is not the conjugal pair, or the nuclear family, but rather the kindred. Whenever any individual loses a spouse, there follows a rearrangement of the balance between kindreds, his own bilateral kindred and his spouse's bilateral kindred, which rearrangement consists in altering the balance between close and spouse's kindred. This flexibility, in the face of what may be termed a demographic change from the point of view of the relational system of kinship, is a property of working class kinship, and doubtless also of American kinship.

We cannot agree with those who would depict kinship systems in the United States as pluralistic in fact or in tendency. And we come to the same conclusion, although for different reasons, as Schneider (1968) did when considering American kinship as a cultural rather than a relational system: essentially there is a single core of kinship in the United States. While Schneider is willing to admit certain amounts of variation in a cultural sense around this single core, we would not go that far with respect to the relational system since the evidence for it is lacking at this point.

Imbalance in Kinship and Relations
Among Parents and Children

As we have just argued, the departure of one of the conjugal partners does not signal that a variant kinship system has emerged. However, in stressing the flexibility of the kinship system as a system we do not mean to imply that it is free of all imbalances, or that from the viewpoint of individual family members kinship and family functions continue to occur in an integrated setting and remain nonproblematical.

Accordingly, we will now address a set of problems in marriage and family relations in order to illustrate what might be termed the costs of system flexibility and also in order to present at least one example of the application of the theoretical perspective developed in this work to some of the concrete issues in the area of marriage and the family. To continue along the lines of the preceding pages, we choose to discuss briefly some problems of socialization and interpersonal relations in single-parent families and in families where certain other kinds of imbalances have developed.

From the point of view of the dependent child in the kindred-based system of kinship relations, the dissolution of the marriage of his parents uncovers a particular kind of stress. The kin-based domestic unit is for him the unit from which bilateral kinship relationships are reckoned. From his point of view in such a unit, both parents' kindred are his consanguines. The kin-based domestic unit is the mechanism by which descendants identify the kinship roles comprising their own kindred. The dissolution of marriage results in a change in the composition of this unit; and marital norms are in this circumstance absent from it.

If the remaining spouse-parent follows the pattern of heightened contact with his or her close kindred and neglects to interact with former spouse's kindred, as our findings would indicate, then the child grows up in a universe which is one-sided, in which social relations and support are seen as coming from half of his or her kindred, and in a household in which one parent is more dominant and is supported by that parent's kindred. Thus, for example, the passivity attributed to males growing up in female-headed households and their ambivalence toward male functions may not only be the result of the absence of an effective male role model. Another significant element in this problem may be the resulting imbalance itself: the mother is perceived by the child as being in a position of power and authority, supported by law and by her own kindred. This is a type of power and authority from which there is no recourse for the child and where there is no counterbalancing from an adult partner.

If children of broken marriages grow up in an imbalanced kinship interaction system, one would not expect that the situation would be remedied by step-kin created by remarriages. One could not expect these people to show the same interest in the children as would representatives of kindred of their missing parent from whom they are isolated. Moreover, remarriage would not necessarily result in replacing a missing parent. From the point of view of the child, the distinction here is between affines and kindred. Step-parents fall into the former not the latter category. Thus, while step-parents may be important, they and the child do not have the same moral bonds of kinship between one another as do children and their bilateral kindred. Naturally these are issues to be better understood by future research. Our point is that the system of kinship relations, in terms of kindred-based linkages, has been neglected in the study of single parent families.

In shifting emphasis now from the single parent family to the marriage which has remained intact, the application of the kindred-based perspective sheds light on some additional dimensions of relations among parents and parents and children. We have seen that upon marriage, equalitarian norms come into play balancing off ego's ties with his kindred with his spouse's ties with hers. Since marriage links but does not necessarily integrate an individual with spouse's kindred, and since there could not be a formal arrangement of reciprocal relations between these two kindred types, there are no mechanisms for adjusting any potentially conflicting positional norms of kinship with those of marriage.

The most immediate consequence of such conflicts are imbalances in the kinship interaction system across the husband-wife relation. These imbalances would affect interpersonal relations in the domestic group—between husband

and wife and between parents and children. In this study we have found that such imbalances are related to age differences and to a high degree of conjugal role segregation. However, one would expect that these differences ramify beyond questions of the division of labor within the household. Farber (1966:72) suggests that when imbalances do occur, one spouse is provided with the means to maintain a position of power, leading to authoritarianism and conflict. Bearing in mind that such means of maintaining power could be enhanced by differentials in the geographical availability of relatives comprising each spouse's kindred, it is apparent why interpersonal family problems assume serious dimensions in such imbalanced kinship situations. Further research is needed to determine how these problems are resolved.

Not only does an imbalanced relational system of kindreds potentially affect the husband-wife bond, but there is some indication that children may be affected as well. A relation of socioemotional solidarity with the kindred of both spouses has been suggested by many as necessary to maintain the type of family interaction conducive to effective socialization. For example, Farber (1966:78) found that couples with emotionally disturbed children tended to favor siblings or cousins of one spouse, or as we would say some members of the close kindred or distant kindred of one spouse, while couples with children who were not emotionally disturbed had a balanced system of kinship interaction.

The absence of symmetrical interaction between each spouse and their respective close and spouse's kindred is thus suggested as a source of personal problems and conflict for the husband and wife.

Moreover, imbalances occurring across the husband-wife bond in relation to kindred and affines are, from the point of view of the child, imbalances within his own kindred. Such imbalances are not conducive to effective socialization. It will be recalled that from ego's perspective, spouse's kindred are affines, and marriage norms govern relations with them. However, from the point of view of ego's children, these same kin are consanguines comprising part of his bilateral kindred. The differential treatment of people who occupy equivalent kinship roles from the point of view of the child and the conflicts that brought this about are thus seen as creating problematic socialization.

If such imbalances follow the child throughout the life cycle, the potential socioemotional and other resources of half of his kindred could be unavailable to him. This potentially disadvantageous situation may well be related to failure to attain educational goals and realize occupational opportunities.

If our views and those of Farber's are correct, then children raised in households where there are imbalances in social relations of the parents' respective kindred may face similar problems that children raised in single parent households confront. If this turns out to be the case, then family disorganization, so called, would not apply to the household per se but to the relational system of kinship.

Bilateral Descent Systems and
Adaptability to Economic Change

To conclude this chapter, we turn our attention to the kindred-based system of kinship and its adaptability in the face of large-scale change impinging upon it from the outside. We wish to close, then, with an issue we raised in the first chapter; an issue which we saw had fundamental implications for modern conceptions and theories of kinship structure in sociology. This is the question of the impact of massive economic change—industrialization—on the structure of kinship and the family.

From the vantage point of the analysis of this book, we can now recognize a pervasive assumption of many of those who address this question. The notion of the lack of adaptability of kinship and family structures underlies much of the thinking of those who consider the fate of family relationships under the impact of the social changes that brought about industrialization and that continue to modernize large parts of the developed as well as underdeveloped areas of the world. The persistence of the idea of the family as a fragile victim of massive economic changes stems from two mistaken ideas concerning kinship: first is the assumption that whenever such a large-scale, economic change as industrialization takes place, its effects fall upon kinship systems of a unitary kind; second, in terms of the effects of economic force upon them, there is essentially no difference between concrete kinship groups on the one hand and social interaction among those related by blood and marriage on the other.

A distinction must be made between unilineal and bilateral kinship systems if we are to understand the effects of basic economic change on kinship and family relations. We have been discussing a bilateral kinship system, one in which descent is traced through both male and female lines. Unilineal kinship systems on the other hand trace descent through either the male or the female line, but not through both. Such systems have the advantage of being able to recruit members for interaction or for group formation in an unambiguous manner. Corporate kinship groups do form easily on the basis of descent through patrilineages or matrilineages. That is, they form easily in comparison with bilateral systems where, by virtue of membership in two lineages, the formation of a discrete kinship unit is accomplished at the expense of one line.

To use an example of Fox's (1967:150), in bilateral descent systems the kin of one lineage could not easily form a residence group because it could only keep all of its members together at the expense of another lineage. Any individual possesses joint memberships, so recruitment on the basis of one lineage deprives another of members. In unilineal systems there is no such structural impediment to the recruitment of discrete units for specific functions. But unilineal systems, while able to form groupings for specific purposes are vulnerable to "demographic fluctuations," to use Fox's phrase.

For instance, the failure of male offspring to be born in one generation would effectively eliminate a patrilineage. Or, serious strains may develop as when ". . . patrilineages each live on a limited amount of land, it is likely that demographic pressures can result in some lineages becoming far too large for the amount of land they hold, while in others the ratio of land to members may drop over a few generations" (Fox, 1967:153). Bilateral systems are more flexible in that many of their members may belong to other kin groupings in which they may take up residence and in this way redistribute themselves among land holdings should such population crises arise. Lack of a corporate kinship group based on a single territory becomes an advantage in the face of social change.

The impact of economic change on unilineal kinship systems is likely to be great. Gough (1961:635-637) gives a graphic picture of the disintegration of matrilineal descent groups. Large unilineal groupings decay and the transition to a bilateral system begins with a narrowing of the span of the effective descent group. As nuclear family units assert their autonomy, conflicts occur within the unilineal group. Eventually, after a transitional period of unknown and doubtless also greatly variable length, the elementary family becomes the significant economic, residential, and socializing unit. Most probably the length of time required for the disintegration of unilineal kinship systems is at least in part dependent on whether they are matrilineal or patrilineal—the latter seemingly are better able to endure the early stages of economic change.

What appears to cause the disintegration of unilineal descent systems is not industrialization per se, although many contemporary examples can be cited showing this process underway in the industrializing areas of the world. Many of the factors which are usually said to have been responsible for the decline of so-called traditional or preindustrial kinship systems, such as stratification by education and socioeconomic rank, geographic and social mobility, and so forth, were not brought into such societies as the accompaniment of the industrialization of the modern era. As Gough (1961:640) states, they could be found in some societies in the fifteenth century, along with trade, the use of money, and markets. It is an economic change of a more fundamental nature than the modern transition to industrialization which is the ultimately responsible economic factor involved in kinship change—for both modern and historical societies—in social systems characterized by unilineal descent. Gough cites Polanyi's (1957:68-69) explanation, namely

". . . the gradual incorporation of the society in a unitary market *system*, in which markets cease to be isolated and are linked in a common standard of value, and in which all produced goods, but more particularly land and other natural resources, and human labor itself, become privately owned and potentially marketable commodities."

What is immediately apparent from this rationale for the disintegration of kinship systems is that by the close of the middle ages many if not all European social systems no longer contained unilineal descent groups, and that bilateral kinship systems probably preceded industrialization in most if not all of those societies in which the Industrial Revolution took hold in the 1800s. In other words, when the period of industrial transformation arrived in the western world, those extended kinship groups which it is alleged to have dissolved by economic requirements for a geographically and socially mobile labor force, by the corrosive influence of universalistic market values on particularistic family values, and by an economic division of labor destructive of small economies tied to family households were not to be found. For in point of fact these kinship groups had already disappeared from most of western European society long before, and whatever effects the industrialization of Europe, and of the United States, may have had, certainly the destruction of groups of extended kin was not one of them.

This is not to imply that social scientists and historians have unraveled the interconnections between industrialization and kinship systems. We still do not have good answers to questions about the nature of the effects of the transition to an industrialized, universalistic society in general, nor to specific questions dealing with its effects on the size of the domestic unit, the extent of kin reckoning, or on social relations among kin. But it is clear that whatever other changes may have been caused by the industrialization of western Europe and the United States, the disintegration of concrete kinship groupings cannot have been among them. Corporate kinship entities such as lineages and clans, characteristic of unilineal systems, had disappeared long before.

The industrialization and modernization of parts of Asia and Africa, and elsewhere, in more recent times has often resulted in the destruction of concrete kinship groupings, since in many of these areas unilineal kinship systems existed. Those who argue that we have inherited a family and kinship system which is the casualty of the Industrial Revolution may have these unilineal systems in mind when they make this judgment. But as far as concrete kinship groupings are concerned, they have perhaps assumed that all the kinship systems affected by industrialization have been of a unitary kind. This is not the case; and our own system of bilateral descent differs as we have seen from unilineal systems in that the only concrete grouping it supports is the nuclear or elementary household.

It has, moreover, become increasingly apparent that the nuclear household was the most common domestic unit in most of Europe prior to the industrial revolution. Parish and Schwartz (1972:170), for example, present convincing quantitative support for this view. It would seem, then, that at least some of the putative consequences of the industrialization of western societies are actually among its antecedents; and that we have been subjected to the blandishments of social mythology as far as the impact of industrialization is concerned. Far from breaking down extended family groups into nuclear family units, it might not be too far-fetched to suggest that industrialization was successful in the West partly because of the prior existence of a compatible form of kinship in many of those countries in which it took hold. The forces of industrialization did not have to overcome the resistances of complex kinship groups such as lineages and clans in these areas.

The second assumption underlying received notions of kinship structure and how it was affected by economic transformation is the idea that concrete kinship groupings are somehow to be equated with extra-familial social interaction among kin. Or, more particularly, that the existence of one presumes the existence of the other and the absence of one presumes the absence of the other. If one makes this assumption, and in addition believes that the arrival of industrialization disintegrated concrete, extended family groups, then it follows that some version of the isolation of the family thesis will be put forward as the typical situation in industrialized societies with respect to interaction among kin.

We take the position that the connection between kinship groups and kinship interaction is neither so inevitable nor so simple. If economic change alters kinship groups, it may not be the case that kinship interaction is altered in the same way. In fact the precise connections between kinship groups and social relations among kin would seem to be an empirical question in any given instance.

We have argued that insofar as concrete kinship groups are concerned, there was little change wrought by industrialization in the West because these groups ceased to exist before that time, and were replaced by domestic units composed mainly of nuclear families. It is therefore most probable that if any major changes in kinship interaction took place during industrialization they were not of the kind that curtailed the social relationships among relatives *because* of the disintegration of more extensive kinship groupings which had previously provided the matrix of interaction among kin. Since in many societies with bilateral kinship systems no concrete kinship groupings were eradicated, the effects of the transition to an industrialized, universalistic society on the nature of extra-familial kin interaction may in all likelihood be negligible.

We take the position that Parsons is correct in his contention that the transition to an industrialized society *can* curtail functions of corporate kinship entities; and we concur with Firth (1956:83) that such entities are not likely to survive as their members disperse into industrial employment and their traditional resources and authority structures lose meaning. However, social interaction among extra-familial kin can be retained on a kinship basis as industrialization proceeds, either in the case where industrialization concomitantly involves a transition from unilineal systems or in the case (such as that of the West in the 1800s) where bilateral kinship systems already existed.

By recognizing the difference between kin groups and social relations, Firth argues that social relations among kin may even be strengthened if the physical isolation of the household is promoted by industrial-urban conditions. According to Firth (1956:83), there is no reason to think that extra-familial kin ties are likely to decline in modern western society. Thus, while recognizing that the nature of our social and cultural emphasis on individual responsibility and personal achievements does not permit us to treat kin as a body in obligation terms, he readily adds that kin can be so treated on a selective basis.

Neither Sussman nor Litwak see Parsons' and Firth's point on this issue. For the imagery and paradigms used by Sussman and Litwak suggest that formal kinship entities can be revitalized with industrialization. They imply that such groups—"modified extended families" or "kin networks"—redefine themselves and their functions, implying that kin are treated as a body in terms of obligations. It is to their discredit that they disagree with Parsons and Firth, because much of the controversy over isolation stems from the failure to see the distinction between formal kinship entities and social relations among kin. A great deal of the confusion in the literature on extra-familial kin ties is a result of Sussman's and Litwak's refusal to give ground on this basic issue.

Despite the fact that the formal organizational structure and functions of kin entities may be curtailed by the requisites of industrialization, extra-familial kin ties are not only retained but have a kinship form. It is in this context that we concur with Wolf (1966:2-7), who argues that social relations among kin in industrializing societies may not have the same functions for the kinship system as such relations in nonindustrialized societies, but that their kinship form is retained. For example, extra-familial ties may occur over a number of kin-related households that in the modern world lack the economic functions present when households were producing units in an economy consisting chiefly of household manufacturing. It is from this point of view that we find that the relational system of kinship in American society has much the same form (while lacking the functions) as that of this system in nonindustrial societies with bilateral descent. The structural form of social relations among kin in societies with bilateral descent has been identified as the kindred—the ego-centered category of socially significant blood relatives. That certain modifications of this basic form of kinship relations have occurred is beyond dispute. They stem from the occupational requisites that geographically disperse the kindred; from an achievement orientation prohibiting us to treat the kindred *as a body* in obligation terms; and from the structural premium placed on the marital bond that makes social relations with affines significant as well. And we have taken as our task in the preceding chapters of this study to spell out that structural form and its modifications, and what they mean for the recruitment of kin for social interaction.

Thus we see that it has been misleading for social scientists to assume that industrialization has wreaked (and still does) its effects on a unitary kinship system. Where economic modernization has taken place in the context of unilineal systems its consequences for kinship and the family have been quite different from those accruing in the context of bilateral systems. The mythology of the impact of industrial change is partly a function of our *correct* observation that massive transformations in kinship occur when unilineal systems bear the brunt of this impact, but our *incorrect* application of this observation to social systems such as our own in which bilateral kinship arrangements predominate.

Yet even this amount of inaccuracy about the nature of economic change and its effects would not have been enough to lead us into error had not another misleading assumption also been made: social scientists have by and large confused concrete kinship groups with the process of interaction among kin. The joint influence of these two assumptions—together with the failure to recognize that in the western European and North American cases, industrialization occurred in bilateral kinship systems in which the only concrete grouping (if one may call it that) is the elementary household, and in which the unit of kinship is the kindred—has led to what must in all honesty be termed intellectual chaos.

At the very least, then, we ought to dispose of the notion that our kinship system and family are fragile entities which are altered in some fundamental way by economic change. If nothing else, bilateral kinship systems and the kinds of family groupings of which they are composed are rather persistent and adaptable social segments. The household groupings in bilateral systems seem to be able to form domiciles of varying degrees of complexity. Parish and Schwartz, examining French census returns ranging from 1856 to 1962, find that even though the nuclear household was and is the predominant domiciliary arrangement there nevertheless persisted on a muted scale, in the agricultural regions of the country, the nineteenth century regional differences in which LePlay's research located concentrations of nuclear, stem, and patriarchal (joint) families. As Parish and Schwartz (1972: 170) state, "In spite of modern communications and transportation, industrialization does not expunge the family traditions of those who remain in agriculture, but only the traditions of those who move to cities and engage in modern work."

Thus in the face of near-universal literacy, and the social context of a modern industrial economy, these differences in household complexity persist. They are, of course, basically differences in the manner in which the inheritance of land, and hence the support of offspring, is handled by families. Bilateral systems of descent seem to permit numerous modes of inheritance, and their concomitant differences in household size and complexity, under the same set of norms governing the reckoning of descent. The range of variation in household complexity, however, has limits. Apparently even LePlay overestimated the extent to which patriarchal households existed, mistaking many large elementary households, with a number of unmarried siblings in residence, for ideal joint families (Parish and Schwartz, 1972: 162).

Appendix A: The Questionnaire

The bulk of the kinship information on which the analysis presented in this book is based was drawn from the following items taken from a larger interview schedule.

	30 Brother	20 Mother	10 Father	80 Husband/wife	50 Son
	38 Brother's wife	21 Grandfather (maternal)	11 Grandfather (paternal)	81 Father-in-law	58 Daughter-in-law
	35 Nephew	22 Grandmother (maternal)	12 Grandmother (paternal)	82 Mother-in-law	55 Son's child
	36 Niece	23 Uncle	18 Stepmother	83 Spouse's brother	60 Daughter
	40 Sister	24 Aunt		84 Spouse's sister	67 Son-in-law
	47 Sister's husband	27 Stepfather		85 Spouse's sister's husband	65 Daughter's child
		25 Half-sibling		86 Spouse's brother's husband	

Now let's talk about your different relatives, where they are, how often you see them, and so on.

152. First of all, do you have any relatives who live on this block, but who don't live here with you? This includes your brothers and sisters, your (wife's/husband's) brothers and sisters, their wives and husbands, their children, etc.

Yes 1
No 2

153. Which relatives are they, and how old is each one? (PRINT QUESTION NO., THE CODE NO. FOR EACH RELATIONSHIP, FIRST NAME AND AGE OF EACH RELATIVE IN COLUMN 1 IN TABLE BELOW) (SHOW R. CARD E)

154. Do you have any relatives who live within 5 blocks of you, but not on this block?

Yes 1
No 2

(IF "YES" REPEAT Q. 153)

155. Do you have any relatives who live within Metropolitan Philadelphia, but not within 5 blocks of you?

Yes 1
No 2

(IF "YES" REPEAT Q. 153)

156. Do you have any relatives elsewhere in the United States?

Yes 1
No 2

(IF "YES" REPEAT Q. 153)

157. Do you have any relatives who don't live in the United States?

Yes 1
No 2

(IF "YES" REPEAT Q. 153)

158. (ASK ONLY OF RELATIVES ON THE SAME BLOCK, *AND* WITHIN 1–5 BLOCKS, *AND* IN METROPOLITAN PHILADELPHIA, IF 30 YEARS OF AGE OR OLDER) What kind of work does he/she do? (Duties and industry)

159. (FOR ONE RELATIVE AT A TIME, ASK Q. 159 THROUGH 162) How often do you usually get together with ____ (RELATIVE) ____ ? (RECORD IN COL. 3 IN TABLE BELOW)

160. How many times during the past 7 days did you get together with ____ (RELATIVE) ____ ? (RECORD IN COL. 4 BELOW)

161. (IF LIVING WITH SPOUSE, ASK:) When you see ____ (RELATIVE) ____ is your husband/wife usually present? (RECORD IN COL. 5 IN TABLE BELOW)

162. Considering all the years you've known ____ (RELATIVE) ____ , including the present year, during what years did you have the *most* contact with him/her? (RECORD IN COL. 6 IN TABLE BELOW)

Q. No.	Name	Relationship Code	Age	Duties	Type of Company	Times Weekly	Times Monthly	Times Yearly	Times Last 7 Days	Yes	No	Years
	Question 153 Column 1			Question 158 Column 2		Question 159 Column 3			Q. 160 Col. 4	Q. 161 Col. 5		Q. 162 Col. 6

Bibliography

Adams, Bert N. KINSHIP IN AN URBAN SETTING. Chicago: Markham Publishing Co., 1968.

_____. "Isolation, Function, and Beyond: American Kinship in the 1960's." JOURNAL OF MARRIAGE AND THE FAMILY 32 (November 1970), pp. 575-597.

Anspach, Donald F. WORKING CLASS KINSHIP INTERACTION. Unpublished doctoral dissertation. Department of Sociology, Case Western Reserve University, 1970.

_____, and George S. Rosenberg. "Working Class Matricentricity." JOURNAL OF MARRIAGE AND THE FAMILY 34 (August 1972), pp. 437-443.

Axelrod, Morris N. "Urban Social Structure and Social Participation." AMERICAN SOCIOLOGICAL REVIEW XXI (February 1956), pp. 13-18.

_____, and H. Sharp. "Mutual Aid Among Relatives in Urban Populations." PRINCIPLES OF SOCIOLOGY. Edited by R. Freedman, et al., New York: Holt and Co., 1956. Pp. 433-439.

Bott, Elizabeth. FAMILY AND SOCIAL NETWORK. London: Tavistock Publications, Ltd., 1957.

Christensen, Harold T. (Ed.). HANDBOOK OF MARRIAGE AND THE FAMILY. Chicago: Rand McNally and Co., 1964.

Codere, Helen. "A Genealogical Study of Kinship in the United States." PSYCHIATRY XVIII (January 1955), pp. 65-79.

Coult, Alan D., and Robert W. Habenstein. "The Study of Extended Kinship in Urban Society." SOCIOLOGICAL QUARTERLY III (April 1962), pp. 141-145.

Cumming, Elaine, and David Schneider. "Sibling Solidarity: A Property of American Kinship." AMERICAN ANTHROPOLOGIST LXIII (June 1961), pp. 498-507.

Davenport, William. "Nonunilinear Descent and Descent Groups." KINSHIP AND FAMILY ORGANIZATION. Edited by B. Farber. New York: John Wiley and Sons, Inc., 1966. Pp. 42-53.

Dotson, Floyd. "Patterns of Voluntary Association Among Urban Working Class Families." AMERICAN SOCIOLOGICAL REVIEW XVI (October 1951), pp. 687-693.

Edwards, John N. (Ed.). THE FAMILY AND CHANGE. New York: Alfred Knopf and Co., 1968.

Farber, Bernard. FAMILY: ORGANIZATION AND INTERACTION. San Francisco: Chandler Publishing Co., 1964.

_____. KINSHIP AND FAMILY ORGANIZATION. New York: John Wiley, 1966.

_____. KINSHIP AND CLASS: A MIDWESTERN STUDY. New York: Basic Books, 1971.

Firth, Raymond (Ed.). TWO STUDIES OF KINSHIP IN LONDON. London: London School of Economic Monographs on Social Anthropology, Number 15, 1956.

_____. "Family and Kinship in Industrial Society." SOCIOLOGICAL RE-VIEW MONOGRAPH, Number 8, 1964, pp. 65-87.

Fox, Robin. KINSHIP AND MARRIAGE: AN ANTHROPOLOGICAL PER-SPECTIVE. London: Nicholls Ltd., 1967.

Freeman, Jesse D. "On the Concept of the Kindred." JOURNAL OF THE ROYAL ANTHROPOLOGICAL INSTITUTE XCI (March 1961), pp. 192-220.

Gibson, Geoffrey. "Kin Family Network: Overheralded Structure in Past Conceptualizations of Family Functioning." JOURNAL OF MARRIAGE AND THE FAMILY 34 (February 1972), pp. 13-23.

Goode, William J. WORLD REVOLUTION AND FAMILY PATTERNS. Glen-coe, Illinois: The Free Press, 1963.

Gough, Kathleen. "The Modern Disintegration of Matrilineal Descent Groups." MATRILINEAL KINSHIP. Edited by D. Schneider and K. Gough. Berkeley: University of California Press, 1961.

Greenfield, Sidney M. "Industrialization and the Family in Sociological Theory." AMERICAN JOURNAL OF SOCIOLOGY LXVII (November 1961), pp. 312-322.

Hays, William L. STATISTICS FOR PSYCHOLOGISTS. New York: Holt, Rinehart, and Winston, 1963.

Homans, George, and David Schneider. "Kinship Terminology and the American Kinship System." AMERICAN ANTHROPOLOGIST LVII (December 1955), pp. 1194-1208.

Irish, Donald P. "Sibling Interaction: A Neglected Aspect of Family Life Research." SOCIAL FORCES XLII (March 1964), pp. 279-288.

Key, William H. "Rural Urban Differences and the Family." SOCIOLOGICAL QUARTERLY II (January 1961), pp. 49-56.

Komarovsky, Mirra. BLUE COLLAR MARRIAGE. New York: Vintage Books Inc., 1962.

Lancaster, Lorraine. "Some Conceptual Problems in the Study of Family and Kin Ties in the British Isles." BRITISH JOURNAL OF SOCIOLOGY XII (December 1961), pp. 317-332.

Litwak, Eugene. "The Use of Extended Family Groups in the Achievement of Social Goals: Some Policy Implications." SOCIAL PROBLEMS VII (Winter 1959-1960), pp. 177-187.

Litwak, Eugene. "Occupational Mobility and Extended Family Cohesion." AMERICAN SOCIOLOGICAL REVIEW XXV (February 1960), pp. 9-21.

_____. "Geographic Mobility and Extended Family Cohesion." AMERICAN SOCIOLOGICAL REVIEW XXV (June 1960), pp. 385-394.

_____. "Extended Kin Relations in an Industrial Democratic Society."

SOCIAL STRUCTURE AND THE FAMILY. Edited by E. Shanas and G. Streib. New Jersey: Prentice-Hall Inc., 1965. Pp. 290-323.

Loudon, J.B. "Kinship and Crisis in South Wales." BRITISH JOURNAL OF SOCIOLOGY XII (December 1961), pp. 333-350.

Mead, Margaret. "The Contemporary American Family As An Anthropologist Sees It." AMERICAN JOURNAL OF SOCIOLOGY 53 (May 1948), pp. 453-459.

Mirande, Alfred M. "The Isolated Family Hypothesis: A Reanalysis." THE FAMILY AND CHANGE. Edited by John N. Edwards. New York: Alfred A. Knopf, 1968.

Mitchell, William E. "Theoretical Problems in the Concept of Kindred." AMERICAN ANTHROPOLOGIST LXV (April 1963), pp. 343-354.

Mogey. John. "Family and Community in Urban-Industrial Societies." HANDBOOK OF MARRIAGE AND THE FAMILY. Edited by Harold Christensen. Chicago: Rand McNally and Co., 1964. Pp. 501-529.

Murdock, George P. SOCIAL STRUCTURE. New York: The Free Press, 1949.

_____. "Cognatic Forms of Social Organization." KINSHIP AND SOCIAL ORGANIZATION. Edited by P. Bohannon and John Middleton. New York: The Natural History Press, 1968. Pp. 235-253.

Parish, Jr., William L., and Moshe Schwartz. "Household Complexity in Nineteenth Century France." AMERICAN SOCIOLOGICAL REVIEW 37 (April 1972), pp. 154-173.

Parsons, Talcott. "The Kinship System of the Contemporary United States." AMERICAN ANTHROPOLOGIST XLV (January-March 1943), pp. 22-38.

_____. THE SOCIAL SYSTEM. Glencoe, Illinois: The Free Press, 1951.

_____. "The Normal American Family." SOURCEBOOK IN MARRIAGE AND THE FAMILY. Edited by Marvin B. Sussman. Boston: Houghton Mifflin Co., 1968. Pp. 36-46.

Petersen, Karen Kay. "Kin Network Research: A Plea for Comparability." JOURNAL OF MARRIAGE AND THE FAMILY XXXI (May 1969), pp. 271-280.

Pitts, Jesse. "The Structural Functional Approach." HANDBOOK OF MARRIAGE AND THE FAMILY. Edited by Harold T. Christensen. Chicago: Rand McNally and Co., 1964. Pp. 51-124.

Reiss, Paul J. "The Extended Kinship System: Correlates of and Attitudes on Frequency of Interaction." JOURNAL OF MARRIAGE AND THE FAMILY XXIV (November 1962), pp. 333-339.

Rivers, William H. SOCIAL ORGANIZATION. New York: Alfred A. Knopf Inc., 1924.

Robins, Lee N., and Miroda Tomanec. "Closeness to Blood Relatives Outside the Immediate Family." JOURNAL OF MARRIAGE AND THE FAMILY XXIV (November 1962), pp. 340-346.

Rodman, Hyman. "Talcott Parsons' View of the Changing American Family."

MARRIAGE, FAMILY, AND SOCIETY: A READER. Edited by Hyman Rodman. New York: Random House, 1965. Pp. 262-286.

Rosenberg, George S. THE WORKER GROWS OLD: POVERTY AND ISOLATION IN THE CITY. San Francisco: Jossey-Bass Inc., 1970

_____, and Donald F. Anspach. "Sibling Solidarity in the Working Class." JOURNAL OF MARRIAGE AND THE FAMILY 35 (February 1973).

Rosow, Irving. "Intergenerational Relationships: Problems and Proposals." SOCIAL STRUCTURE AND THE FAMILY: GENERATIONAL RELATIONS. Edited by Ethel Shanas and Gordon F. Streib. Englewood Cliffs, New Jersey: Prentice-Hall, Inc., 1965, pp. 341-378.

Schneider, David M. "Some Muddles in the Models: Or, How the System Really Works." THE RELEVANCE OF MODELS FOR SOCIAL ANTHROPOLOGY. Edited by Michael Banton. London: Tavistock Publications, 1965. Pp. 25-85.

_____. AMERICAN KINSHIP: A CULTURAL ACCOUNT. New Jersey: Prentice-Hall Inc., 1968.

_____, And Kathleen Gough (Eds.). MATRILINEAL KINSHIP. Berkeley: University of California Press, 1961.

Shanas, Ethel, and Gordon F. Streib (Eds.). SOCIAL STRUCTURE AND THE FAMILY: GENERATIONAL RELATIONS. New Jersey: Prentice-Hall Inc., 1965.

Sussman, Marvin B. "The Help Pattern in the Middle Class Family." AMERICAN SOCIOLOGICAL REVIEW XVIII (January 1953), pp. 22-28.

_____. "The Isolated Nuclear Family: Fact or Fiction?" SOCIAL PROBLEMS VI (Spring 1959), pp. 333-340.

_____, and L.G. Burchinal. "Kinship Family Network: Unheralded Structure in Current Conceptualizations of Family Functioning." JOURNAL OF MARRIAGE AND THE FAMILY XXIV (August 1962), pp. 231-240.

_____. "Relationships of Adult Children with Their Parents in the United States." SOCIAL STRUCTURE AND THE FAMILY: GENERATIONAL RELATIONS. Edited by Ethel Shanas and Gordon F. Streib. New Jersey: Prentice-Hall Inc., 1965. Pp. 65-92.

_____. "The Urban Kin Network in The Formulation of Family Theory." Paper presented at the Ninth International Seminar on Family Research, Tokyo, Japan, 1965.

Turner, Christopher. FAMILY AND KINSHIP IN MODERN BRITAIN. London: Routledge and Kegan Paul, 1969.

Winch, Robert F., Scott A. Greer, and Rae L. Blumberg. "Ethnicity and Extended Familism in an Upper Middle Class Suburb." AMERICAN SOCIOLOGICAL REVIEW XXXII (April 1967), pp. 267-272.

_____, and Scott A. Greer. "Urbanism, Ethnicity, and Extended Familism." JOURNAL OF MARRIAGE AND THE FAMILY XXX (February 1968), pp. 40-45.

Wolf, Eric R. "Kinship, Friendship, and Patron-Client Relations in Complex Societies." THE SOCIAL ANTHROPOLOGY OF COMPLEX SOCIETIES. Edited by Michael Banton. New York: Frederick A. Praeger, 1966. Pp. 1-22.

Young, Michael, and Peter Willmott. FAMILY AND KINSHIP IN EAST LONDON. London: Routledge and Kegan Paul, 1957.

Zelditch, Morris. "Cross-Cultural Analysis of Family Structure." HANDBOOK OF MARRIAGE AND THE FAMILY. Edited by Harold T. Christensen. Chicago: Rand McNally and Co., 1964. Pp. 462-500.

Index of Names

About the Authors

George S. Rosenberg is Professor of Sociology at Case Western Reserve University, where he also directs the Social Gerontology Training Program in the Sociology Department. He is the author of *The Worker Grows Old: Poverty and Isolation in the City* and has contributed numerous articles to professional journals. He received his PhD from Columbia University. His research interests are in stratification, gerontology and kinship. He is presently studying the impact of economic centralizations, such as the European Economic Community, on the future of British class structure.

Donald F. Anspach is Assistant Professor of Sociology at the University of Maine at Portland-Gorham. He received his PhD from Case Western Reserve University. He specializes in stratification, family and social theory and has published in professional journals. He is continuing his research on kinship in a study of occupational succession and mobility among relatives in Maine coastal fishing communities.